3A

PATHWAYS

SECOND EDITION

Reading, Writing, and Critical Thinking

MARI VARGO

LAURIE BLASS

D1569255

NATIONAL GEOGRAPHIC
LEARNING

Australia • Brazil • Mexico • Singapore • United Kingdom • United States

NATIONAL GEOGRAPHIC
LEARNING

Pathways
Reading, Writing, and Critical Thinking
Split 3A, **Second Edition**

Mari Vargo and Laurie Blass

Publisher: Andrew Robinson

Executive Editor: Sean Bermingham

Development Editor: Melissa Pang

Director of Global Marketing: Ian Martin

Product Marketing Manager: Tracy Bailie

Media Researcher: Leila Hishmeh

Senior IP Analyst: Alexandra Ricciardi

IP Project Manager: Carissa Poweleit

Senior Director of Production: Michael
  Burggren

Senior Production Controller: Tan Jin Hock

Manufacturing Planner: Mary Beth Hennebury

Art Director: Brenda Carmichael

Compositor: MPS North America LLC

Cover Photo: A rock moves across the
  Racetrack Playa in California's Death Valley
  National Park: © KiskaMedia/iStock/Getty
  Images

For product information and technology assistance, contact us at
Cengage Learning Customer & Sales Support, cengage.com/contact

For permission to use material from this text or product,
submit all requests online at **cengage.com/permissions**
Further permissions questions can be emailed to
permissionrequest@cengage.com

Split 3A:
ISBN-13: 978-1-337-62331-5

Split 3A with Online Workbook:
ISBN-13: 978-1-337-62492-3

National Geographic Learning
20 Channel Center Street
Boston, MA 02210
USA

National Geographic Learning, a Cengage Learning Company, has a mission to bring the world to the classroom and the classroom to life. With our English language programs, students learn about their world by experiencing it. Through our partnerships with National Geographic and TED Talks, they develop the language and skills they need to be successful global citizens and leaders.

Locate your local office at **international.cengage.com/region**

Visit National Geographic Learning online at **NGL.Cengage.com/ELT**
Visit our corporate website at **www.cengage.com**

Printed in China
Print Number: 03   Print Year: 2020

Contents

Scope and Sequence

Critical Thinking	Writing	Vocabulary Extension
Focus Analyzing Evidence Evaluating Evidence, Reflecting, Synthesizing	**Skill Focus** Writing Body Paragraphs **Language for Writing** Making Comparisons **Writing Goal** Writing two body paragraphs comparing animal and human behavior	**Word Link** *pre-*
Focus Analyzing Levels of Certainty Evaluating, Synthesizing	**Skill Focus** Writing a Summary **Language for Writing** Paraphrasing **Writing Goal** Writing two summaries	**Word Link** *-ist*
Focus Analyzing Quotes Justifying Your Opinion, Evaluating, Synthesizing	**Skill Focus** Writing Introductory and Concluding Paragraphs **Language for Writing** Using the Simple Past and the Present Perfect **Writing Goal** Writing a problem-solution essay about how a city solved a problem it faced	**Word Partners** Expressions with *income*
Focus Inferring Applying, Analyzing Evidence	**Skill Focus** Writing a Process Essay **Language for Writing** Using Parallel Structures **Writing Goal** Writing a process essay about how people can prepare for a natural hazard	**Word Forms** Changing Nouns and Adjectives to Verbs with *-en*
Focus Evaluating Arguments Synthesizing, Evaluating/ Justifying	**Skill Focus** Writing a Cause-Effect Essay **Language for Writing** Using *if . . . , (then) . . .* **Writing Goal** Writing a cause-effect essay about the positive and negative effects of tourism on a place	**Word Forms** Adjectives and Nouns ending in *-ive*

Pathwats Reading, Writing, and Critical Thinking, Second Edition uses National Geographic stories, photos, video, and infographics to bring the world to the classroom. Authentic, relevant content and carefully sequenced lessons engage learners while equipping them with the skills needed for academic success. Each level of the second edition features **NEW** and **UPDATED** content.

Academic skills are clearly ▶ labeled at the beginning of each unit.

ACADEMIC SKILLS

READING   Identifying arguments and counterarguments
WRITING   Writing a persuasive essay
GRAMMAR   Describing visual information
CRITICAL THINKING   Evaluating visual data

NEW AND UPDATED ▶ reading passages incorporate a variety of text types, charts, and infographics to inform and inspire learners.

Explicit reading skill instruction ▶ includes main ideas, details, inference, prediction, note-taking, sequencing, and vocabulary development.

▼ **Critical thinking activities** are integrated throughout each unit, and help develop learner independence.

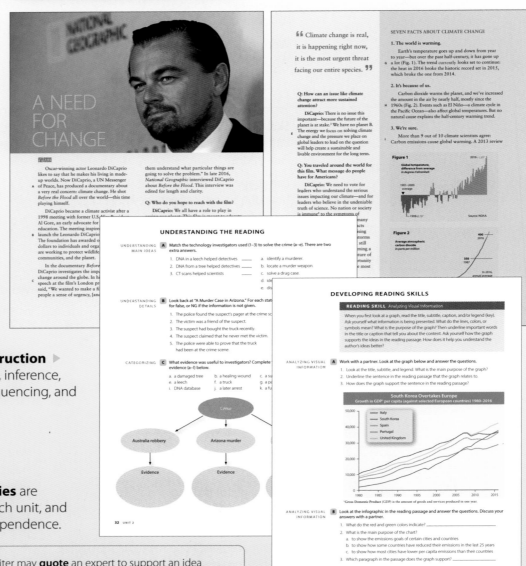

CRITICAL THINKING   A writer may **quote** an expert to support an idea presented in an article. When you read a quote from an expert, ask yourself: Which of the writer's main or supporting ideas does the quote support?

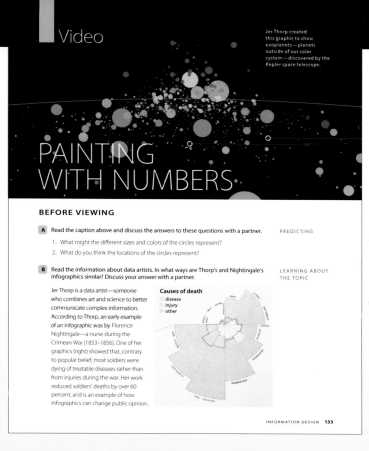

Jer Thorp created this graphic to show exoplanets—planets outside of our solar system—discovered by the Kepler space telescope.

PAINTING WITH NUMBERS

BEFORE VIEWING

A Read the caption above and discuss the answers to these questions with a partner.   PREDICTING

1. What might the different sizes and colors of the circles represent?
2. What do you think the locations of the circles represent?

B Read the information about data artists. In what ways are Thorp's and Nightingale's infographics similar? Discuss your answer with a partner.   LEARNING ABOUT THE TOPIC

Jer Thorp is a data artist—someone who combines art and science to better communicate complex information. According to Thorp, an early example of an infographic was by Florence Nightingale—a nurse during the Crimean War (1853–1856). One of her graphics (right) showed that, contrary to popular belief, most soldiers were dying of treatable diseases rather than from injuries during the war. Her work reduced soldiers' deaths by over 60 percent, and is an example of how infographics can change public opinion.

Causes of death
- disease
- injury
- other

INFORMATION DESIGN **133**

◀ **NEW AND UPDATED *Video*** sections use National Geographic video clips to provide a bridge between Readings 1 and 2, and to give learners ideas and language for the unit's writing task.

◀ **NEW** An additional short reading passage provides integrated skills practice.

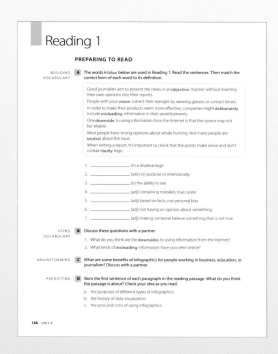

Reading 1

PREPARING TO READ

BUILDING VOCABULARY   **A** The words in blue below are used in Reading 1. Read the sentences. Then match the correct form of each word to its definition.

Good journalists aim to present the news in an **objective** manner without inserting their own opinions into their reports.

People with poor **vision** correct their eyesight by wearing glasses or contact lenses.

In order to make their products seem more effective, companies might **deliberately** include **misleading** information in their advertisements.

One **downside** to using information from the Internet is that the source may not be reliable.

Most people have strong opinions about whale hunting. Not many people are **neutral** about the issue.

When writing a report, it's important to check that the points make sense and don't contain **faulty** logic.

1. _____ (n) a disadvantage
2. _____ (adv) on purpose or intentionally
3. _____ (n) the ability to see
4. _____ (adj) containing mistakes; inaccurate
5. _____ (adj) based on facts, not personal bias
6. _____ (adj) not having an opinion about something
7. _____ (adj) making someone believe something that is not true

USING VOCABULARY   **B** Discuss these questions with a partner.

1. What do you think are the **downsides** to using information from the Internet?
2. What kinds of **misleading** information have you seen online?

BRAINSTORMING   **C** What are some benefits of infographics for people working in business, education, or journalism? Discuss with a partner.

PREDICTING   **D** Skim the first sentence of each paragraph in the reading passage. What do you think the passage is about? Check your idea as you read.

a. the purposes of different types of infographics
b. the history of data visualization
c. the pros and cons of using infographics

126 UNIT 6

VOCABULARY EXTENSION   UNIT 1

WORD LINK *pre-*

Words that begin with the prefix *pre-* mean "before in time." For example, *previously* means "before the time period that you are talking about." *Pre-* can be added to some common root words. For example, *preview* means "to see a part of something before watching the whole thing."

Complete each sentence with the words below. One word is extra.

predict	prepare	preschool	prevent	preview	previous

1. It is a good idea to _____ some slides before giving a presentation.
2. Scientists are developing apps that can _____ a person's behavior better than a human can. For example, the app can tell if a customer will buy a product again.
3. For many entry-level jobs, no _____ experience is required.
4. To _____ conflict in a workplace, try to avoid aggressive behavior with your co-workers.
5. Movie companies often upload a short video online to give people a _____ of an upcoming movie and get them excited about it.

VOCABULARY EXTENSION   UNIT 2

WORD LINK *-ist*

Some nouns that end in *-ist* can refer to someone who works in a specific academic or professional field. An *archaeologist*, for example, works in the field of archaeology. In general, for words ending in a vowel or *-y*, drop the vowel or *-y* and add *-ist*.

Complete each sentence with the correct noun form of the underlined word.

1. Someone who writes novels is a _____
2. Someone who produces art is an _____
3. Someone who looks at how the economy works is an _____
4. Someone who provides therapy to other people is a _____
5. Someone who plays the piano as a job is a _____

VOCABULARY EXTENSION **243**

▲ **Key academic and thematic vocabulary** is practiced, and expanded throughout each unit.

▲ **NEW Vocabulary extension activities** cover word forms, word webs, collocations, affixes, and more, to boost learners' reading and writing fluency.

Writing Skills Practice

Pathways' approach to writing guides students through the writing process and develops learners' confidence in planning, drafting, revising, and editing.

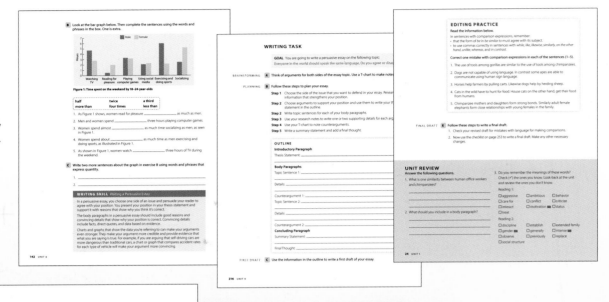

Writing Goals and *Language for Writing* sections provide the focus and scaffolding needed for learners to become successful writers.

An **online workbook**, powered by MyELT, includes video clips and automatically graded activities for learners to practice the skills taught in the Student Books.

UPDATED Revising Practice sections incorporate realistic model paragraphs and help learners refine their writing.

NEW Guided online writing ractice provides reinforcement and ...lidation of language skills, helping ... become stronger and more ...ters.

SOCIAL RELATIONSHIPS 1

Polar bear cubs stay with their
mothers for more than two years.

ACADEMIC SKILLS

READING	Identifying main and supporting ideas
WRITING	Writing body paragraphs
GRAMMAR	Making comparisons
CRITICAL THINKING	Analyzing evidence

THINK AND DISCUSS

1 Aside from humans, what other animals live
in social groups?
2 What similarities do you think there are between
human relationships and animal relationships?

EXPLORE THE THEME

A **Read the information on these pages and answer the questions.**

   1. What are some examples of nonhuman primates?

   2. What similarities have researchers discovered between humans and other primates?

B **Match the words in blue to their definitions.**

treat (v) to behave toward someone in a particular way

Interact (v) to communicate with someone or something

Care · for (v) to look after someone (usually a young, sick, or old person)

Families of wild macaques often bathe in the hot springs in Yamanouchi, Japan.

SOCIAL ANIMALS

Researchers have discovered that humans share certain behavioral characteristics with other primates—the group of mammals that includes humans, monkeys, and apes.

Basic Communication

Primatologists—scientists who study primates—have found that some apes are capable of basic communication using human sign language. Researchers have also observed apes inventing and using tools to get food and complete other tasks.

Social Behavior

Both humans and other primates tend to live in social groups, and they share some characteristics in terms of their social behavior. Researchers today are looking at the similarities and differences in how humans and animals interact within their own social groups, for example, how they treat each other and care for their young.

Reading 1

PREPARING TO READ

BUILDING
VOCABULARY

A The words in **blue** below are used in Reading 1. Read the paragraph. Then match the correct form of each word to its definition.

Most workplaces are positive environments where people work well together. However, an **aggressive** employee in an office can easily lead to workplace stress—by treating coworkers unfairly, **criticizing** them, or taking credit for their work. Employees who experience workplace **conflict** on a regular basis can lose **motivation** to do good work. Why do some employees not cooperate with their coworkers? It may be that the employee is **ambitious** and thinks that aggressive **behavior** will help them get ahead. Or the employee is afraid of losing **status** in the company and thinks that aggressive behavior will help them stay on top.

1. _Conflict_ (n) a serious disagreement
2. _behavior_ (n) the way someone acts
3. _Aggressive_ (adj) acting in a forceful or competitive way
4. _motivation_ (n) a feeling of being excited to do something
5. _Criticizing_ (v) to speak badly of someone or something
6. _Ambitious_ (adj) wanting to be successful
7. _Status_ (n) an individual's position within a group

USING
VOCABULARY

B Discuss these questions with a partner.

1. How **ambitious** are you? Would you rather be a president of a company, or a low-level or mid-level employee without a lot of responsibilities? Why?
2. How would you react to an **aggressive** coworker? Give an example.

BRAINSTORMING

C Discuss your answers to these questions in groups.

1. In what ways do you think employees cooperate in the workplace? Give two examples.
2. In what ways do you think primates cooperate in the wild? Give two examples.

PREDICTING

D Read the title, headings, and captions in the reading passage. How do you think human behavior in the office is similar to primate behavior in the jungle? Write three ideas. Then check your ideas as you read.

_____

_____

_____

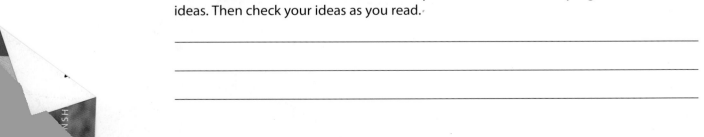

THE APE
IN THE OFFICE

🎧 1.01

A   **Does the "office jungle" mirror behavior in the real jungle? New research shows people in offices may use conflict and cooperation in similar ways to primates in the jungle.**

B   Animal behavior specialist Richard Conniff is the author of *The Ape in the Corner Office*. In his book, Conniff examines corporate behavior through the eyes of a primatologist. He suggests cooperation is the key to success for both humans and other primates. He sees similarities in the ways they use social networks and hierarchies[1] to gain status. He also points out that while conflict can be effective at times, both humans and apes usually prefer to cooperate.

---

[1] **Hierarchies** are groups or situations that are organized from higher to lower by rank, social status, or function.

COOPERATION VERSUS CONFLICT

C People often think that the animal world is full of conflict. However, conflict and aggression actually play a smaller role in the wild than cooperation. In fact, according to Conniff, both humans and other primates are social creatures, and both groups normally try to avoid conflict. Chimpanzees, for example, typically spend their days caring for their young and traveling together in small groups. Conniff points out that chimps spend about 5 percent of the day being aggressive, but 15 to 20 percent of the day grooming[2] each other. For humans and other primates, conflict is rare and does not last long. For both species, cooperation is a more effective way to succeed and survive.

THE VALUE OF NETWORKING

D Research also shows that people and other primates use similar social networking strategies to get ahead in life. They create tight social bonds by sharing resources, doing each other favors, building teams, and making friends. Employees with ambitious career goals, for example, often rely on powerful people in their office to help them get better jobs. In a similar way, chimps work to strengthen relationships with other chimps.

E Frans de Waal, a primatologist at Emory University in Atlanta, Georgia, claims that for chimps, "you can never reach a high position in their world if you don't have friends who help you." In fact, research shows that chimps often create bonds to strengthen their status, or importance, in the community. They do favors for one another and share resources. They sometimes also use their cunning[3] to get ahead. "In chimps a common strategy is to break up alliances that can be used against them," de Waal explains. "They see a main rival sitting with someone else and they try to break up [that meeting]."

Aggressive behavior may bring results, but also leads to isolation for the aggressor.

[2] **Grooming** is the activity of animals cleaning each other.
[3] **Cunning** is the ability to achieve things in a clever way, often by deceiving other people.

THE IMPORTANCE OF HIERARCHIES

Mein Idea

F

Groups of coworkers and primate groups have similar social rules. In both cases, the groups organize themselves into hierarchies, and individual members know their roles. Individuals in both human and ape groups have a particular position in relation to other group members. This decides their behavior in the group. For example, young people may speak softly or avoid eye contact when they talk to people with higher status. Similarly, Conniff explains that when chimpanzees approach a powerful or senior member, they try to make themselves look as small as they can.

THE LIMITS OF AGGRESSION

G

Although cooperation is more common in groups, both humans and other primates sometimes use conflict in order to gain status. Aggressive behaviors get attention, and they show an individual's power in the group. People sometimes shout or intimidate others to make a point or win an argument. Apes show aggression by pounding their chests, screeching, or hitting trees. However, Conniff notes that conflict does not gain long-term success for either species. When bosses criticize their employees, treat them unfairly, or make their working lives difficult, employees become stressed, lose motivation, and quit their jobs. When apes are aggressive, they chase other apes away. In both cases, aggressive individuals can become isolated, and neither humans nor apes want to be alone.

H

In his book, Conniff makes the case that interacting in a kind and polite way is more beneficial for both humans and primates. "The truth is we are completely dependent on other people emotionally as well as for our physical needs," Conniff concludes. "We function as part of a group rather than as individuals." Employees who cooperate in the office and primates who cooperate in the wild find themselves happier, more effective, and more likely to survive.

UNDERSTANDING THE READING

UNDERSTANDING PURPOSE

A According to the reading passage, what were the two main reasons Conniff wrote *The Ape in the Corner Office*? Check (✓) the most suitable answers.

☑ 1. to explain how apes and humans behave similarly

☐ 2. to show how humans have learned from animal behavior

☐ 3. to argue that animals cooperate better than humans do

☑ 4. to show how humans and other primates value cooperation

SUMMARIZING

B Complete the summary below. Write no more than one word in each space.

People in offices and primates in the wild both prefer to ¹ *cooperative* with one another and avoid ² *conflict* . They also use social ³ *networking* skills to be successful. Both groups organize themselves into ⁴ *hierarchies* , which affect how they behave in a group. While uncommon, both office workers and primates sometimes use ⁵ *aggressive* behavior to assert themselves.

CATEGORIZING

C Complete the Venn diagram with examples (a–j) from the reading passage describing human and other primate behavior.

a. speak softly or avoid eye contact

b. share resources

c. do favors

d. build teams

e. groom one another

f. travel together in groups

g. do well in groups

h. pound chests, screech, or hit trees

i. rely on powerful people to get better jobs

j. reduce body size to look smaller

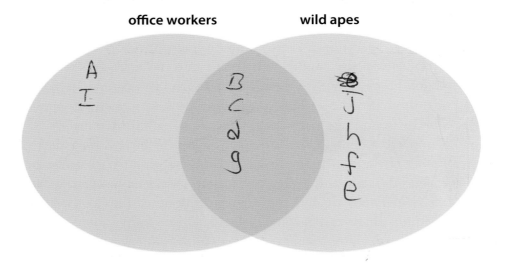

office workers   wild apes

A   B   e
I   C   j
             d   h
             g   f
                          e

CRITICAL THINKING When a writer is making a claim or an argument, it is important to **analyze the evidence** (examples, statistics, research, etc.) that they provide. As you read, think about and evaluate the evidence mentioned. Does this evidence clearly support the writer's main ideas?

D What evidence does the writer use in the passage to support their main idea in each section? Complete the chart with the key points of evidence.

Section	Evidence
Cooperation versus Conflict	Statistics:
The Value of Networking	An expert / Research:
The Importance of Hierarchies	An example:
The Limits of Aggression	An example:

E Work in groups. Look at the evidence in exercise D. Based on the evidence provided, which section do you think is the least convincing? Why?

F Find and underline the following words in the reading. Use context to identify their meanings. Then circle the correct options to complete the definitions.

bonds (paragraph D)	intimidate (paragraph G)
rival (paragraph E)	beneficial (paragraph H)

1. If an interaction is *beneficial*, it is **useless / useful.**

2. A *rival* is someone you are **cooperating / competing** with.

3. If you *intimidate* people, you make them feel **frightened / happy** enough to do what you want them to do.

4. If you have strong *bonds* with someone, you feel very **connected to / distant from** them.

G Work with a partner. Can you think of two examples from your own experience that either support or contradict the ideas expressed in the reading?

_____

_____

DEVELOPING READING SKILLS

READING SKILL Identifying Main and Supporting Ideas

The main idea of a paragraph is the most important idea, or the idea that the paragraph is about. It is often, but not always, stated in the first sentence. Supporting ideas help to explain the main idea. They answer questions about the main idea, such as how, why, what, and when. As you read, it is helpful to identify the main ideas of paragraphs in a passage, and distinguish them from supporting ideas.

Which of these sentences best expresses the main idea of paragraph C of Reading 1?

a. Both primates and humans tend to spend more time being cooperative than they do fighting with one another.

b. Chimpanzees typically spend their days traveling together and taking care of one another.

Sentence **a** best expresses the main idea of the paragraph. Sentence **b** expresses a supporting idea: It helps to explain the main idea by providing an example.

IDENTIFYING MAIN AND SUPPORTING IDEAS

A Read the following paragraph about gorilla behavior. Is each sentence (1–4) a main idea or a supporting idea? Write **M** for Main Idea or **S** for Supporting Idea. One is extra.

M Scientists have found that male gorillas in the forests of northern Congo splash water to help them find a mate. Richard Parnell, a primate researcher at the University of Stirling, observed that male gorillas intimidate other males and try to get the attention of females by splashing water with their hands. In one type of splashing behavior, for example, male gorillas raise one or both arms and hit the surface of the water with their palms open. Using water in this way, Parnell says, shows that gorillas are "adaptable, innovative, and intelligent creatures."

_____ 1. Male gorillas sometimes hit the water with their palms open.

_____ 2. Parnell says that splashing proves that gorillas are capable creatures.

_____ 3. Splashing water helps scare off other males.

___S___ 4. Larger male gorillas are usually more successful at finding mates.

M Main idea ___ 5. A study shows that male gorillas splash water to attract female gorillas.

IDENTIFYING MAIN AND SUPPORTING IDEAS

B Look at your answers to exercise A. How do you know which sentences are supporting ideas? What questions (why, how, where, what) do they answer about the main idea? Discuss with a partner.

APPLYING

C Look back at paragraph G of Reading 1. Underline a main idea of the paragraph and two ideas that support it.

Video

ELEPHANT ORPHANS

A shelter in Kenya cares for young elephants that have lost their parents.

BEFORE VIEWING

A Read the photo caption. What kind of care do you think the elephant orphans need? Discuss with a partner.

PREDICTING

B Read the information about the illegal ivory trade and answer the questions. Then discuss them with a partner.

LEARNING ABOUT THE TOPIC

One of the biggest dangers facing African elephants is hunting by poachers—people who illegally catch or kill animals for profit. Poachers kill elephants so they can remove and sell their valuable ivory tusks. Ivory is usually made into jewelry and art objects. Although the ivory trade is banned in most countries, ivory is often smuggled[1] in and sold illegally. Between 2010 and 2012, poachers killed over 100,000 African elephants. In Central Africa, the elephant population has decreased by 64 percent in a decade. Poachers have shortened these animals' life spans and disrupted their close communities.

[1]**smuggled:** brought into or out of another country or area illegally

1. Why do you think people continue to buy objects made of ivory?

   Because it's made in to jewelry and art.

2. What do you think could be done to stop the illegal ivory trade?

   I think thy ponple from africa needs mono guibe or garts aso po protect elephonts.

C The words in **bold** are used in the video. Read the paragraph. Then match the correct form of each word to its definition.

The David Sheldrick Wildlife Trust in Nairobi, Kenya, takes care of orphan elephants. Many of these elephants are orphans because poachers **slaughtered** their mothers. **Caretakers** at the Trust stay with the orphans 24 hours a day, in order to provide them with plenty of **maternal** interaction. The organization's goal is the **reintroduction** of the elephants back into the wild.

1. ~~Caretakers~~ slaughtered maternal (adj) like a mother
2. Slaughtered (v) to kill in large numbers
3. Caretakes (n) a person responsible for looking after someone or something
4. reintroduction (n) the act of putting something back into an environment where it once was

WHILE VIEWING

A ▶ Watch the video. What is one of the biggest challenges that the David Sheldrick Wildlife Trust faced in keeping the baby elephants alive? Circle the best answer.

a. getting them to trust humans
b. keeping them warm
c. learning what to feed them

B ▶ Watch the video again. Write answers to the following questions.

1. According to the video, what are two things baby elephants need?
   Care and right milk formula

2. What is one way caretakers try to copy an elephant's relationship with its mother?
   Mother elephants stay closed to their children

3. What are three ways human and elephant babies are similar?
   Young elephants like to play, so social and Emotional life to human

AFTER VIEWING

A Discuss these questions with a partner.

1. At the end of the video, the narrator says, "These orphans are all safe here—for the time being." Why do you think the narrator uses the phrase "for the time being"?
   narrator she's trying to say always bright future

2. How effective do you think elephant orphanages are in addressing the issue of poaching? Why?
   It's effictive to elephant's because they have feeings too. They wants to be saved

B Write one behavior that both primates and elephants have in common with humans. Use information from the video and Explore the Theme.
   Social behavior like grooming together

Reading 2

PREPARING TO READ

BUILDING VOCABULARY

A The words and phrases in **blue** below are used in Reading 2. Read the sentences. Then match the correct form of each word or phrase to its definition.

> Researchers have **observed** that children **generally** sleep better when parents **establish** a regular bedtime routine.
>
> **Previously**, it was common for **extended families** to live together in one home. But today, fewer people live with their grandparents or other relatives.
>
> Coyotes and wolves have similar **social structures**—both live in family groups.
>
> It's normal for children, regardless of **gender**, to have an **intense** feeling of fear when they are separated from their parents. These strong feelings often go away with time.
>
> One way to **discipline** children is to send them to their rooms alone.
>
> When animals shed their fur, new fur grows to **replace** the fur that is lost.

1. _Previously_ (adv) usually
2. _intense_ (adj) very great or extreme
3. _extended family_ (n) a group that includes uncles, cousins, grandparents, etc.
4. _extended families_ _social structure_ (n) the way a group of people or animals is organized
5. _genders_ (n) the characteristics of being male or female
6. _Establish_ (v) to create or start something that will last a long time
7. _discipline_ (v) to train someone to follow rules or codes of behavior
8. _observed_ _Observe_ (v) to notice something after looking closely
9. _replacement_ (v) to have something new or different instead of the original
10. _previously_ (adv) before the time period that you are talking about

USING VOCABULARY

B Discuss these questions with a partner.

1. What are two ways in which **establishing** a routine can make your life easier?
2. What are some benefits of living in an **extended family**? What are some drawbacks?

PREDICTING

C Read the title and the subheadings in the reading passage. What links the three stories together? Check your idea as you read.

a. male and female roles in animal societies
b. scientific research of primates in Africa
c. animal societies in which females have power

GENDER IN THE WILD

🎧 1.02

A   **How does gender impact family relationships in the wild? Recent studies show how gender influences the social structure of elephants, geladas, and chimps.**

Studies Show Gender Effect in Elephant Societies

B   Young elephants grow up in extended matriarchal[1] families. Elephant mothers, aunts, grandmothers, and female friends cooperate to raise babies in large, carefully organized groups. This system helps protect young orphan elephants when hunters or farmers kill their mothers. When a young elephant is orphaned, other females take over the dead mother's role. The strong bonds between females continue throughout their lives, which can be as long as 70 years. In contrast, young male elephants stay close to their female family members until they are 14. Then they generally leave their mothers and form other groups with male elephants.

C   Previously, male elephants were perceived to be less social than females. However, a recent study at Etosha National Park in Namibia shows that males often form intense, long-lasting friendships with other males. During

---

[1] In a **matriarchal** family or group, the rulers are female and power is passed from mother to daughter.

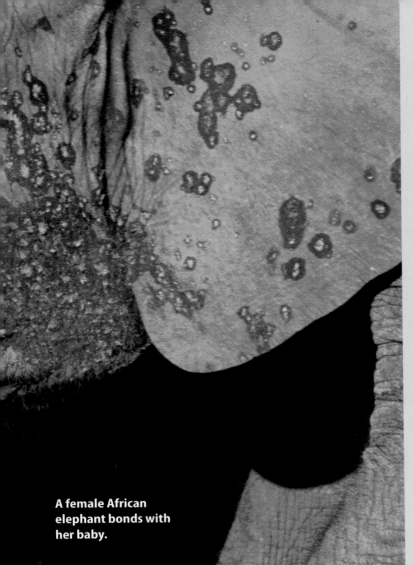

A female African elephant bonds with her baby.

Gelada Study Reveals Female Primates with Power

Geladas are primates that live in the remote highlands of Ethiopia. Males are larger than females, but females have the real power in family groups. Wildlife biologist Chadden Hunter studies geladas in Simen Mountains National Park in Ethiopia. Hunter has observed that typical family units have between **D** two and eight adult females, their offspring, and a primary male, which researchers call the family male. Gelada males have little say in what the family does from day to day. The females decide where and how long to graze[3] for food, when to move, and where to sleep. They also choose which male will be their mate and when it is time to replace that mate.

Young bachelor[4] males live in separate groups. They spend most of their time observing family groups and looking for **E** opportunities to challenge the family males. When a young bachelor comes too close to a family, the family male chases him away.

[3] When animals **graze**, they eat the grass or other plants that are growing in a particular place.
[4] A **bachelor** is a single male without a female partner or children.

the study, Stanford University behavioral psychologist Caitlin O'Connell-Rodwell found that each member knew his status, and that the group followed a strict social hierarchy. Older males act as teachers and mediators[2] for younger ones, controlling or disciplining them when conflict occurs. These strict rules of behavior are helpful when food and drink are scarce. O'Connell-Rodwell observed that "in dry years, the strict pecking order they establish benefits all of them." For example, the young bulls know they must get in line behind the more senior elephants. In this way, everyone gets a turn to eat and drink, conflict is avoided, and peace is maintained.

[2] A **mediator** is someone who helps two people or groups solve an issue or a problem.

In gelada societies, females are the real decision-makers.

Young female chimps may care for sticks like mother chimps care for their babies.

To replace a family male, the females invite a bachelor into the family. Females typically do this when a family male becomes weak or does not give enough attention to them or their offspring. Hunter explains, "That's especially true in families where there are six or seven females; it's a lot of work to keep them all happy."

Hunter has observed that no family male lasts more than four years, and many are replaced before three. However, replaced males do not leave their families. Rather, they stay on in a kind of grandfather role. "That way, they can protect their children," he says, "and they're very aggressive about that." Hunter's study has generated new interest in geladas, and it will challenge primatologists to learn more about their gender behavior.

F

Researchers Discover Gender-Driven Play in Chimps

G Just as human children often choose different toys, some monkeys in captivity have demonstrated gender-driven toy preferences. For example, young female vervet and rhesus monkeys often play with dolls in captivity, while young males prefer toys such as trucks. Now, for the first time, a study in Kibale National Park in

Uganda shows that the same is true for chimps in the wild.

Richard Wrangham, a primatologist at Harvard University, has been studying the play behavior of male and female chimps. His team observed that the way a community of young Kanyawara female chimps played with sticks mimicked caretaking behaviors. The young females took sticks to their nests and cared for them like mother chimps with their babies. The

H chimps appeared to be using the sticks as dolls, as if they were practicing for motherhood. This play preference, which was very rarely seen in males, was observed in young female chimps more than a hundred times during 14 years of study. In contrast, young males did not normally play with objects. Instead, they preferred active play—climbing, jumping, and chasing each other through trees.

I Stick play may have evolved to prepare females for motherhood. It may have given them an advantage by providing skills and knowledge that contributed to their survival. It is also possible that stick play is just an expression of the imagination—an ability found in chimps and humans but few other animals.

UNDERSTANDING THE READING

A Choose the sentence that best expresses the main idea of each section in the passage.

UNDERSTANDING MAIN IDEAS

1. **Studies Show Gender Effect in Elephant Societies**

   a. Both male and female elephants have an excellent memory and are able to remember elephants they meet.

   (b) Female elephants are in charge of raising families, while males form hierarchical groups with other males.

2. **Gelada Study Reveals Female Primates with Power**

   (a.) Female geladas control family groups in gelada society.

   b. There is a strict hierarchy within female geladas in a single family.

3. **Researchers Discover Gender-Driven Play in Chimps**

   a. The types of play that young chimps prefer seem to be related to gender.

   b. Young chimps learn their social skills by playing with their mothers.

B Complete the main ideas (M) and supporting ideas (S) from "Gelada Study Reveals Female Primates with Power." Write no more than three words in each space.

IDENTIFYING MAIN AND SUPPORTING IDEAS

Paragraph D

M: Female geladas have _the real power_ in family groups.

   S1: Family groups have a large number of geladas.
   S2: Female geladas decide what the family does _how long to graze_
   S3: Female geladas choose their _mate and when to replace mate._

Paragraph E

M: Nonfamily male geladas live in _seperate groups._
   S1: Bachelor males wait for a chance to challenge the _the family males_
   S2: Female geladas _can or replace a_ bachelor males when they want to.

Paragraph F

M: Most family males are _replaced_ after a few years.
   S: The old family males _protects thier offspring_ in the family group.

C Complete each sentence with details from the reading passage. Write no more than three words in each space.

UNDERSTANDING DETAILS

Studies Show Gender Effect in Elephant Societies

1. In male elephant groups, each member knows his _status_.

2. _Older Male elefents_ discipline young male elephants when they fight.

Gelada Study Reveals Female Primates with Power

3. In a typical gelada family, there is one _family Male._

4. When the family male is replaced, he usually takes on a _grandfather_ role.

Researchers Discover Gender-Driven Play in Chimps

5. Young females play with sticks, while young males tend to prefer _to play with trucks._

6. Playing with sticks may prepare young female chimps for _Motherhood_

D What evidence does the author use in "Researchers Discover Gender-Driven Play in Chimps"? Complete the statements below. Then discuss your ideas with a partner.

1. The article describes a _Toy_ in Kibale National Park as evidence for gender-driven play in chimps.

2. The expert who did the chimp study is Richard Wrangham, a _primatoligist_ from Harvard University.

3. Wrangham's team observed that female chimps' stick play was similar to _their mothers_ behaviors.

4. Wrangham's study lasted _14_ years. During this time, his team observed the same behavior more than _100_ times.

chimps

E Discuss these questions with a partner.

1. Do you think the supporting evidence in exercise D is convincing? Why or why not?
I think it's supporing because it shows the time of the _gerada_

2. Compare the three reports in the passage. Which one do you think provides the most convincing supporting evidence? Why?
I think the 1st one support the most becase it tells about the sexter and clarify the things.

F Find and underline these words and phrases in the passage. Use context to identify their meanings. Then complete the sentences with a suitable form of the words and phrases.

> pecking order (paragraph C)   in captivity (paragraph G)
> offspring (paragraph D)   mimicked (paragraph H)

1. Hyenas live in groups with a strict _pecking order_. One female has the most power and makes all of the decisions for the group.

2. Researchers saw that a baby chimp _mimicked_ her mother's behavior.

3. A mother emperor penguin protects her _offspring_ from the Antarctic cold by keeping it under a warm layer of feathered skin.

4. It is difficult to study animals in the wild, but it is easy to study animals _in captivity_.

G Compare the animal species you learned about in this unit. Check (✓) the column(s) that apply to each species. Discuss the reasons for your answers with a partner.

Species	Females Control the Group	Hierarchy Is Important	Forming Strong Bonds Is Important
chimpanzees		✓	
elephants			✓
geladas	✓		

Writing

EXPLORING WRITTEN ENGLISH

A Read the sentences below. Write **S** for sentences that show similarities. Write **D** for sentences that show differences.

NOTICING

1. _**S**_ As both humans and other primates tend to live in social groups, they may share some characteristics in terms of their social behavior.

2. _**S**_ Young people may speak softly or avoid eye contact when they are talking to people with higher status. Similarly, when chimpanzees approach a powerful or senior member, they try to make themselves look smaller.

3. _**D**_ A male gorilla usually has the power in a gorilla family group. In contrast, females make the decisions in a gelada family group.

4. _**D**_ Human boys and girls often choose different toys. Likewise, young chimps in captivity have shown gender-driven toy preferences.

5. _**D**_ Unlike young female chimps, young males did not normally play with objects.

LANGUAGE FOR WRITING Making Comparisons

Use these expressions to show similarities.

*Office workers **are similar** to primates. **Both** use conflict and cooperation in groups.*

*Humans generally live in harmony. **Likewise / Similarly**, chimpanzees try to avoid conflict.*

***Like** humans, chimpanzees may limit aggression to avoid isolation.*

Use these expressions to show differences.

***While** aggression is part of normal primate behavior, it plays a limited role in the wild.*

*The strong bonds among female elephants continue throughout their lives. **In contrast**, young male elephants stay close to their female family members only until they are 14.*

*Elephant families are matriarchal. **On the other hand**, males traditionally have the power in gorilla groups.*

*Young male elephants live with their female family members, **whereas** older males form their own groups.*

***Unlike** young male chimps, who prefer active play, young female chimps have a preference for playing with sticks.*

Note:

• The form of *be* in *be similar to* must agree with its subject.

• Use *likewise* and *similarly* at the beginning of sentences, followed by a comma.

• *In contrast* and *on the other hand* can appear at the beginning of sentences, followed by a comma. They can also appear after the subject. Note the use of commas in this case: *Males, on the other hand, traditionally have the power in many human cultures.*

B Underline the words and phrases in exercise A that show similarities and differences.

C Complete the sentences with suitable words or phrases for making comparisons. Add commas if necessary.

1. Female geladas hold the power in the family. _____But,_____ males have little say about what goes on in the family.

2. Social networking is important in the human workplace. _____Likewise,_____ chimpanzees form strong bonds within their groups.

3. Male geladas are big and have bushy manes _____whereas,_____ female geladas are small and less distinctive-looking.

4. Young male chimps prefer active play. Young female chimps _____Unlike,_____ prefer less active play.

5. Humans have invented tools to help them survive. _____while,_____ chimpanzees make and use tools for specific purposes.

D Use the expressions in the Language for Writing box to write three sentences comparing elephants, chimpanzees, and geladas. Use the information from the chart in exercise G in Understanding the Reading 2.

Geledas ~~have~~ female have more power them male Geledas. But elephants make their Strong bond with their families. Whereas, chimpanzees hierarchy is important to them.

WRITING SKILL Writing Body Paragraphs

An essay is a piece of writing that presents information and ideas on a topic. It typically has the following structure:

Introductory paragraph ⟶ Body paragraphs ⟶ Concluding paragraph

You will learn more about the introductory and concluding paragraphs in Unit 3. An essay has two or more **body paragraphs**. Each one expresses one main idea. A good body paragraph includes a topic sentence that presents the paragraph's main idea. It also includes supporting ideas that develop the main idea. Explanations, details, and examples give further information about the supporting ideas.

In a comparison essay, one way to organize body paragraphs is the point-by-point method. With this method, you discuss one **point of comparison** in each paragraph. For example, in an essay comparing wolves and dogs:

Body paragraph 1   the animals' relationships with humans

Body paragraph 2   the social structures of both animals

Below are typical ways to organize body paragraphs for a comparison essay:

Body paragraph 1		**Body paragaph 2**
a similarity	⟶	another similarity
a difference	⟶	another difference
a similarity	⟶	a difference

E Read the body paragraph below. Answer the questions and then discuss your answers with a partner.

One way that dogs and wolves differ is in their relationships with humans. Dogs are generally friendly and helpful around humans. This is probably because they have been living closely with humans for thousands of years. No one knows exactly why early wolves (ancestors of dogs) approached humans and began living with them, but these tamer individuals gradually evolved into the dogs we know today. Over time, dogs and humans developed a mutually beneficial relationship: humans sheltered and fed dogs, and dogs did jobs for humans. For example, dogs helped early humans hunt. Wolves, on the other hand, are shy and fearful of humans. One reason for this is that wolves are generally afraid of anything that is unfamiliar. This tendency most likely evolved as a survival strategy. Anything unfamiliar in a wolf's environment is a potential danger, so this fear helps it avoid threats to its existence. As a result, wolves are less likely to interact with humans.

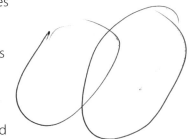

1. Does the body paragraph focus mainly on a similarity or a difference?

    _____

2. Read the following thesis statement. Which of the two points of comparison does the body paragraph explain? Underline it.

    *While wolves and dogs are similar in some ways, the two animals are different in terms of **their relationships with humans** and **their social structures**.*

3. In the paragraph above, underline and label:
    a. the topic sentence
    b. a supporting idea about dogs
    c. a supporting idea about wolves
    d. an example that shows dogs' relationship with humans
    e. an explanation for wolves' behavior

The ancestors of the Mexican wolf were likely the first wolves to arrive in North America.

WRITING TASK

GOAL You are going to write two body paragraphs on the following topic:

Think about an animal in this unit or another animal that is similar to humans in some way. What is one way its behavior is similar to and different from human behavior?

BRAINSTORMING **A** Choose an animal that is similar to humans in some way. Write notes about the animal's behavior. For example, what is its social hierarchy like? How are gender roles different?

PLANNING **B** Follow these steps to make notes for your body paragraphs.

Step 1 From your notes, choose two points of comparison to write about.

Step 2 Complete the first thesis statement if both your points of comparison are on similarities or both are on differences. Complete the second thesis statement if they are one of each.

Step 3 Write a topic sentence for each body paragraph.

Step 4 Add supporting ideas and details (examples, explanations, etc.) for each point.

main Idea   Details

Subbating Idea?

example

OUTLINE

Thesis Statement

1. While _monkeys_ and _human_ are similar / different in some ways, the two are different / similar in terms of their _Knows faces_ and _Tickled laugh_.

2. _monkeys_ and _human_ are similar in some ways but different in others. They both _____, but they differ in terms of _____.

Body Paragraph 1

Topic Sentence: _Similarly are that_ _____

Supporting Ideas / Details: _____

Body Paragraph 2

Topic Sentence: _Dissimuls_ _____

Supporting Ideas / Details: _____

FIRST DRAFT **C** Use the information in your outline to write a first draft of your body paragraphs.

REVISING PRACTICE

The drafts below are the second body paragraph for the thesis statement in exercise E on page 21.

What did the writer do in Draft 2 to improve the paragraph? Match the changes (a–d) to the highlighted parts.

a. added a supporting detail
b. corrected language for making comparisons

c. added a topic sentence
d. deleted unrelated information

Draft 1

Wolves in the wild live in social groups called "packs." A wolf pack is made up of a male and female "alpha" pair—the leaders of the pack—and the alpha pair's offspring and extended family. Most wolves live in the United States, Canada, and Russia. Wolves live this way mainly because they have to hunt for their food, and packs hunt more successfully than individuals. Their clear hierarchy helps them cooperate in hunts and avoid fighting over food within the group. Unlike wolves need to live in packs, dogs do not. This is because, unlike wolves, dogs do not need to hunt to survive. Dogs in the wild search for food scraps left by humans or other animals on their own. Domestic dogs are fed by their human owners. Even when two or more dogs live together in a house, there is no alpha in the group. The dogs deal with conflict on a case-by-case basis, and any member of the group can breed.

Draft 2

Another way that wolves and dogs differ is in their social structures. Wolves in the wild live in social groups called "packs." A wolf pack is made up of a male and female "alpha" pair—the leaders of the pack—and the alpha pair's offspring and extended family. Wolves live this way mainly because they have to hunt for their food, and packs hunt more successfully than individuals. Their clear hierarchy helps them cooperate in hunts and avoid fighting over food within the group. The alphas eat first, make all the decisions for the pack, and are the only ones in the pack that breed. While wolves need to live in packs, dogs do not. This is because, unlike wolves, dogs do not need to hunt to survive. Dogs in the wild search for food scraps left by humans or other animals on their own. Domestic dogs are fed by their human owners. Even when two or more dogs live together in a house, there is no alpha in the group. The dogs deal with conflict on a case-by-case basis, and any member of the group can breed.

D Now use the questions below to revise your paragraphs. REVISED DRAFT

☐ Does your thesis statement state your points of comparison?

☐ Do your body paragraphs relate to the thesis statement?

☐ Do both body paragraphs have clear topic sentences?

☐ Do your supporting ideas and details relate to the main idea of each body paragraph?

EDITING PRACTICE

Read the information below.

In sentences with comparison expressions, remember:
- that the form of *be* in *be similar to* must agree with its subject.
- to use commas correctly in sentences with *while, like, likewise, similarly, on the other hand, unlike, whereas,* and *in contrast.*

Correct one mistake with comparison expressions in each of the sentences (1–5).

1. The use of tools among gorillas are similar to the use of tools among chimpanzees.

2. Dogs are not capable of using language. In contrast some apes are able to communicate using human sign language.

3. Horses help farmers by pulling carts. Likewise dogs help by herding sheep.

4. Cats in the wild have to hunt for food. House cats on the other hand, get their food from humans.

5. Chimpanzee mothers and daughters form strong bonds. Similarly adult female elephants form close relationships with young females in the family.

FINAL DRAFT **E** Follow these steps to write a final draft.

1. Check your revised draft for mistakes with language for making comparisons.

2. Now use the checklist on page 253 to write a final draft. Make any other necessary changes.

UNIT REVIEW
Answer the following questions.

1. What is one similarity between human office workers and chimpanzees?

_____

_____

_____

2. What should you include in a body paragraph?

_____

_____

_____

3. Do you remember the meanings of these words? Check (✔) the ones you know. Look back at the unit and review the ones you don't know.

Reading 1:

☐ aggressive   ☐ ambitious   ☐ behavior

☐ care for   ☐ conflict   ☐ criticize

☐ interact   ☐ motivation [AWL]   ☐ status

☐ treat

Reading 2:

☐ discipline   ☐ establish   ☐ extended family

☐ gender [AWL]   ☐ generally   ☐ intense [AWL]

☐ observe   ☐ previously   ☐ replace

☐ social structure

SCIENCE AND INVESTIGATION 2

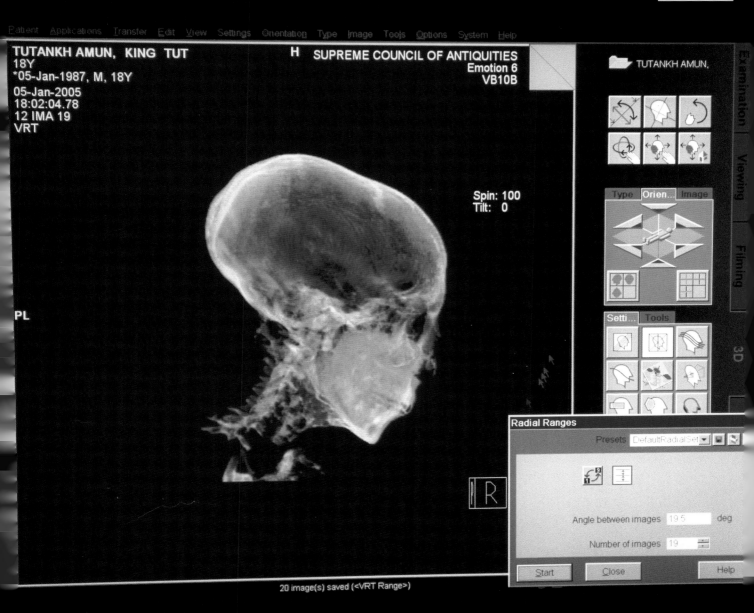

Patient Applications Transfer Edit View Settings Orientation Type Image Tools Options System Help

TUTANKH AMUN, KING TUT
18Y
*05-Jan-1987, M, 18Y

05-Jan-2005
18:02:04.78
12 IMA 19
VRT

H SUPREME COUNCIL OF ANTIQUITIES
Emotion 6
VB10B

Spin: 100
Tilt: 0

PL

R

20 image(s) saved (<VRT Range>)

Radial Ranges

Presets DefaultRadialSet

Angle between images 19.5 deg

Number of images 19

Start   Close   Help

TUTANKH AMUN,

Examination | Viewing | Filming | 3D

Type | Orien... | Image

Setti... | Tools

**Researchers use a CT scanner
to look inside the body of
Tutankhamun.**

ACADEMIC SKILLS

READING Identifying a sequence of events

WRITING Writing a summary

GRAMMAR Paraphrasing

CRITICAL THINKING Analyzing levels of certainty

THINK AND DISCUSS

1 In what ways can technology help
investigators solve crimes?

2 Do you know of any crimes that were solved
using technology?

A **Look at the information on these pages and discuss the questions.**

   1. What can DNA phenotyping tell us about a person?

   2. What *can't* DNA phenotyping tell us about a person?

B **Match the correct form of the words in blue to their definitions.**

_____ (n) a person who the police think may be guilty of a crime

_____ (v) to carry out (usually something illegal or bad)

_____ (v) to find out something by researching or calculation

PUTTING A FACE TO A CASE

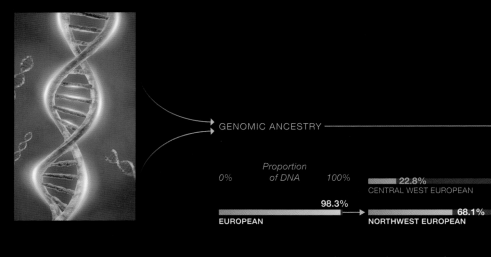

GENOMIC ANCESTRY

Proportion
of DNA
0%   100%

22.8%
CENTRAL WEST EUROPEAN

98.3%

68.1%
NORTHWEST EUROPEAN

EUROPEAN

1. A DNA sample is first scanned.

2. A computer makes predictions about a person's traits, such as ancestry, eye color, or skin color.

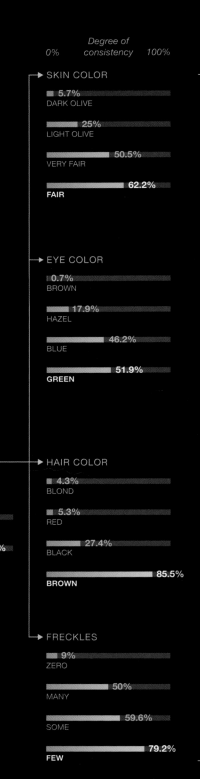

Degree of
0%   consistency   100%

SKIN COLOR

5.7%
DARK OLIVE

25%
LIGHT OLIVE

50.5%
VERY FAIR

62.2%
FAIR

EYE COLOR

0.7%
BROWN

17.9%
HAZEL

46.2%
BLUE

51.9%
GREEN

HAIR COLOR

4.3%
BLOND

5.3%
RED

27.4%
BLACK

85.5%
BROWN

FRECKLES

9%
ZERO

50%
MANY

59.6%
SOME

79.2%
FEW

DNA—a tiny molecule found in almost every part of a person's body—contains a code that gives the body instructions for the growth of cells. Except for the DNA of identical twins, every person's DNA is unique. Because each person's DNA is distinctive, it is a valuable tool for identification. For several years, police have used DNA to identify victims of crimes—and to **determine** who may have **committed** them.

Scientists have also developed a new technique called DNA phenotyping. This technique can determine a person's eye color, their natural hair color, the possible shapes of their facial features, and their geographic ancestry. With this information, technicians can create a picture or a 3-D model of what a person might look like. However, DNA phenotyping cannot determine a person's age, weight, or whether they have a beard or dyed hair. Because this technique can only provide clues about a person's appearance, it cannot necessarily be used to positively identify criminals. However, it can help police rule out **suspects**.

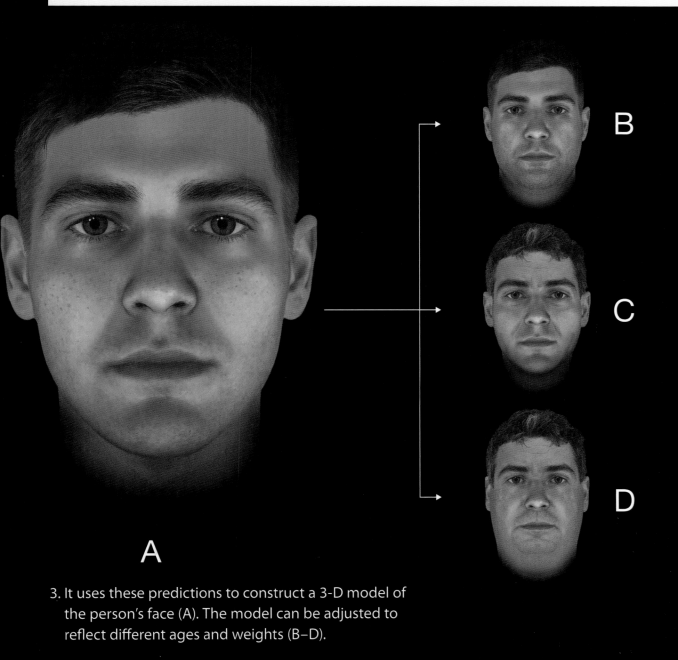

A

B

C

D

3. It uses these predictions to construct a 3-D model of the person's face (A). The model can be adjusted to reflect different ages and weights (B–D).

Reading 1

PREPARING TO READ

BUILDING
VOCABULARY **A** The words in **blue** below are used in Reading 1. Read the paragraphs. Then match each word to its definition.

CT Scanning

A CT scanner is a medical imaging device that can take 3-D images of the inside of almost any object. With it, a doctor can **examine** the inside of a patient's body without cutting the patient open. This technology can **reveal** conditions that aren't easily known, such as tumors, infections, and internal bleeding. CT scanners can also help police to find evidence, and scientists to solve **mysteries** about the past.

Fingerprinting

Every person on Earth has a different fingerprint pattern. Even if you cut or burn your fingers, the same fingerprint pattern will grow back when the injury **heals**. Fingerprint **analysis** can help police **detectives** solve crimes. For example, fingerprints collected at a crime scene can help **prove** that a particular person has been to that location.

1. _____ (v) gets better; becomes healthy

2. _____ (v) to uncover something that is hidden

3. _____ (n) things that are impossible to explain or understand

4. _____ (n) people whose job is to solve crimes

5. _____ (v) to look closely at something

6. _____ (n) the process of studying something carefully

7. _____ (v) to show that something is true or accurate

USING
VOCABULARY **B** Discuss these questions with a partner.

1. What skills do you think police **detectives** need to have? Why?

2. Would you be good at investigating a crime or **mystery**? Why or why not?

PREDICTING **C** Skim the first paragraph and the subheadings in the reading passage. What kinds of crime cases will you read about? How might technology be useful for these types of investigations? Discuss with a partner. Then check your ideas as you read the passage.

_____

_____

TECH DETECTIVES

🎧 1.03

A Police detectives have always made use of the latest technologies to solve crimes. As three cases show, modern technology can help scientists and detectives understand and solve mysteries both from the present and from the past.

A ROBBERY[1] CASE IN AUSTRALIA

B When most people think of leeches, they imagine disgusting blood-sucking worms that they would prefer to avoid. However, leeches can actually be useful. In fact, in 2009, detectives in Australia were able to use a leech to solve an eight-year-old robbery case. In 2001, two men robbed a 71-year-old woman in her home in the woods in Tasmania, stealing several hundred dollars. The men escaped, but soon

after, detectives investigating the crime scene found a leech filled with blood. The detectives thought that the leech could have attached itself to one of the robbers in the woods. It might have sucked the robber's blood while he was traveling through the woods, and then fallen off during the robbery. The detectives extracted some DNA from the blood in the leech and kept it in their database.[2]

C Eight years later, police arrested a suspect on an unrelated drug charge. As part of his examination, his DNA was analyzed and it matched that taken from the leech. This proved that the suspect was at the scene of the crime. After the police questioned him, the suspect eventually admitted to committing the 2001 robbery.

[1] A **robbery** is the crime of stealing money or property, often using force.

[2] A **database** is a collection of data or information that is stored in a computer.

Palo verde flowers

A MURDER CASE IN ARIZONA

The first conviction[3] based on plant DNA evidence occurred in the state of Arizona, in the United States. When a murder was committed in 1992 in the state capital, Phoenix, police found a pager[4] at the scene of the crime that led them to a suspect. The suspect admitted to giving the victim a ride in his truck, but denied any wrongdoing. In fact, he claimed that she had actually robbed him, which is why his pager was found at the crime scene. Forensic[5] investigators examined his truck and found seed pods, which were later identified as the fruits of the palo verde tree. And indeed, a palo verde tree at the scene of the crime looked like a truck might have hit it.

However, this evidence alone was not enough. An investigator wondered if it was possible to link the exact tree at the crime scene with the seed pods found on the truck. A geneticist at the University of Arizona in Tucson showed that it was. Individual plants—in this case, palo verde trees—have unique patterns of DNA. Through DNA analysis of the seed pods, the geneticist determined that its DNA matched the one on the truck. This proved that the truck had definitely been to the crime scene and had collided with one specific tree—thus contradicting the suspect's story. With this information, it was possible to convict the suspect of the crime.

A BODY IN THE MOUNTAINS

Europe's oldest mummy,[6] now known as the Iceman, was discovered by hikers in the frozen ice of the Italian Alps in 1991. Scientists believe he lived about 5,300 years ago in an area north of what is now Bolzano, Italy. Wounds on the Iceman's body clearly show that he died a violent death. But CT imaging technology has helped scientists piece together even more clues about the life and death of this ancient Neolithic[7] human.

CT imaging identified an arrowhead buried in the Iceman's left shoulder, indicating that he was shot from behind. Scientists also discovered a wound on one of his hands. This told them that he had likely been in a fight and that his enemies later chased after and killed him. While this may be true, close analysis of this hand injury shows that the wound was already beginning to heal at the time of his death. So it is unlikely he injured his hand in his final days. Moreover, a later study of the CT images revealed that the Iceman had a full stomach at the time he was killed. This meant that he ate a big meal immediately before his death—not something a person would do if enemies were chasing him. Scientists guessed that the Iceman might have been resting after a meal when enemies attacked him from behind.

Perhaps the most likely explanation is that the Iceman was fleeing an earlier battle, but thought he was safe at the moment of his murder. Scientists continue to analyze the Iceman using the latest technology to find more clues to history's oldest murder mystery.

---

[3] If someone has a **conviction**, they are found guilty of a crime in a court of law.

[4] A **pager** is an electronic device that is used for contacting someone.

[5] A **forensic** investigation involves the use of scientific methods and techniques to solve crimes.

[6] A **mummy** is a dead body that was preserved long ago, usually by being rubbed with special oils and wrapped in cloth.

[7] If something is **Neolithic**, it is from the last part of the Stone Age.

An artist's view of the Iceman's final moments: An arrowhead discovered in the Iceman's left shoulder indicates that he was shot from behind and was probably unaware of his killers.

UNDERSTANDING THE READING

UNDERSTANDING
MAIN IDEAS

A Match the technology investigators used (1–3) to solve the crime (a–e). There are two extra answers.

1. DNA in a leech helped detectives __D__
2. DNA from a tree helped detectives __a__
3. CT scans helped scientists __e__

a. identify a murderer.
b. locate a murder weapon.
c. solve a drug case.
d. identify a thief.
e. discover how a man was murdered.

UNDERSTANDING
DETAILS

B Look back at "A Murder Case in Arizona." For each statement below, circle T for true, F for false, or NG if the information is not given.

1. The police found the suspect's pager at the crime scene. (T) F NG
2. The victim was a friend of the suspect. T (F) NG
3. The suspect had bought the truck recently. T (F) (NG)
4. The suspect claimed that he never met the victim. T F (NG)
5. The police were able to prove that the truck had been at the crime scene. (T) F NG

CATEGORIZING

C What evidence was useful to investigators? Complete the diagram with the pieces of evidence (a–l) below.

a. a damaged tree   b. a healing wound   c. a suspect's blood   d. an arrowhead
e. a leech   f. a truck   g. a pager   h. seed pods
i. DNA database   j. a later arrest   k. a full stomach   l. tree DNA

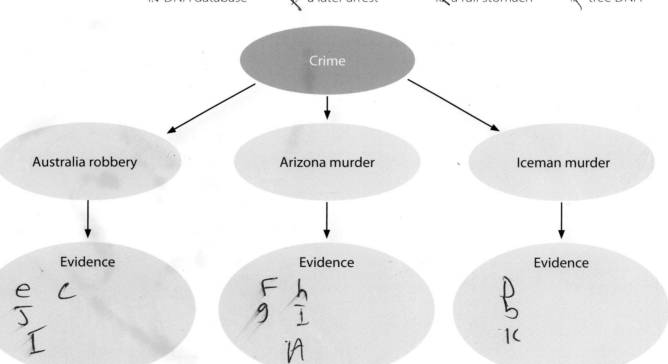

Crime

Australia robbery   Arizona murder   Iceman murder

Evidence   Evidence   Evidence

e c   F h   b
j   g   i   c
I   A

CRITICAL THINKING   As you read, look for words and phrases that help you
analyze levels of certainty about information in the passage.

Words that indicate the information is factual or certain:
definitely, know, prove, clearly, show, and *this means*

Words that indicate the information is mostly certain:
believe, probably, suggest that, argue that, and *likely/unlikely*

Words that indicate the information is not certain:
possibly, could, might, perhaps, and *maybe*

D Read these sentences from "A Body in the Mountains." How certain is the writer about
each underlined piece of information? Rate them (3 = very certain; 2 = mostly certain;
1 = not certain). Then share the reasons for your answers with a partner.

CRITICAL THINKING:
ANALYZING
CERTAINTY

1. _2_   Scientists believe <u>he lived about 5,300 years ago in an area north of what is</u>
   <u>now Bolzano, Italy</u>.

2. _3_   Wounds on the Iceman's body clearly show that <u>he died a violent death</u>.

3. _3_   Close analysis of this hand injury shows that <u>the wound was already</u>
   <u>beginning to heal at the time of his death</u>.

4. _2_   So it is unlikely <u>he injured his hand in his final days</u>.

5. _3_   This meant that <u>he ate a big meal immediately before his death</u> …

6. _1_   Scientists guessed that <u>the Iceman might have been resting after a meal</u>
   <u>when enemies attacked him from behind</u>.

7. _2_   Perhaps the most likely explanation is that <u>the Iceman was fleeing an earlier</u>
   <u>battle, but thought he was safe at the moment of his murder</u>.

E Look at "A Robbery Case in Australia" and "A Murder Case in Arizona." In each section,
find a piece of information that is more certain and one that is less certain. Share your
ideas with a partner.

CRITICAL THINKING:
ANALYZING
CERTAINTY

A robbery case in Aus is more certain becaus
of the blood matches. A murder ase in
Arizona is about the plant of tree

F Based on the evidence in the reading passage and your own ideas, what do you think
happened to the Iceman, e.g., who he was with, why he was killed, why his body was
left there? Make some notes below. Then discuss with a partner.

CRITICAL THINKING:
EVALUATING

DEVELOPING READING SKILLS

READING SKILL Identifying a Sequence of Events

When you are trying to understand an article about a crime or a mystery, look for certain words and phrases in the story to help you understand the sequence, or order, of events.

Time markers such as days, months, years, and times of day:

on Monday	*in March*	*in 1991*	*at 5:30*

Words that indicate that one event happened **before** another event:

before	*earlier*	*(one year) ago*	*already*

Words that indicate that one event happened **after** another event:

later	*after*	*now*	*once*

Words and phrases that indicate that two events occurred **at the same time**:

at the time of	*at that moment*	*at the same time*	*while*

Words and phrases that indicate that something happened **much earlier**:

a long time ago	*for some time*	*in ancient (times)*	*in prehistoric (times)*

ANALYZING **A** Scan the section "A Robbery Case in Australia." Underline words and phrases that indicate when events happened.

IDENTIFYING A SEQUENCE **B** Now use information from "A Robbery Case in Australia" to complete the timeline below.

a. Police arrested a suspect on a drug charge.

b. The suspect admitted that he committed the robbery.

c. Police analyzed the drug charge suspect's DNA.

d. Two men entered a house to rob the woman who lived there.

e. The leech fell off of the robber.

f. Detectives found a leech filled with blood in the house.

g. Detectives took blood out of the leech.

h. Detectives matched the DNA from the leech with the DNA of the suspect.

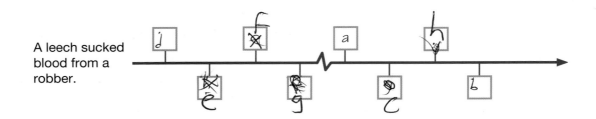

A leech sucked blood from a robber.

Video

The Iceman's body was found at this spot in the Ötzal Alps.

SECRETS IN THE ICE

BEFORE VIEWING

A Read the information about the Iceman and answer the questions below.

LEARNING ABOUT THE TOPIC

- The Iceman was wearing a coat, a belt, leggings, and shoes, all made of leather. The shoes were waterproof and designed to help the wearer walk in snow. He was carrying tools, weapons, and two baskets of medicinal plants.

- Scientists believe that the Iceman was about 46 years old and five feet two inches (about 1.58 meters) tall. He had medium-length wavy dark hair and brown eyes.

- He had 61 tattoos, mostly consisting of parallel lines. These are the oldest tattoos ever found, and prove that tattooing has existed much longer than previously thought.

- Researchers have found 19 living relatives of the Iceman in Austria. These people and the Iceman likely share an ancestor who lived 10,000 to 12,000 years ago.

1. What information about the Iceman do you think was easily visible? What information do you think was gained using technology?

   _____

   _____

2. What three things about the Iceman do you still want to know?

   _____

   _____

B The words in **bold** below are used in the video. Read the sentences. Then match the correct form of each word to its definition.

> Because the Iceman was frozen, he was perfectly **preserved**.
>
> Studying the Iceman can give us **insights** into life 5,000 years ago. For example, we can learn about the clothes people wore in the ancient past.
>
> Studying the contents of the Iceman's stomach may tell us a lot about how **nutrition** affected his health.
>
> An analysis of his **genes** shows that he and 19 people in Austria share an ancestor.

1. _____ (n) the right diet for healthy growth
2. _____ (v) to keep in a good state
3. _____ (n) an accurate understanding of something
4. _____ (n) a part of DNA that contains the information for the physical characteristics of a person, animal, or plant

WHILE VIEWING

A ▶ Watch the video. According to Albert Zink, what makes the Iceman so special? Check (✓) the correct answers.

☐ 1. He can help us improve DNA technology.

☐ 2. He is the oldest mummy in Europe.

☐ 3. He is perfectly preserved.

☐ 4. He helps us understand how people lived in those places.

☐ 5. He gives us information about diseases.

☐ 6. He carried tools that were technologically advanced for his time.

B ▶ Watch the video again. What does Albert Zink still hope to discover about the Iceman? Note two things.

_____

_____

AFTER VIEWING

A Do you think it is right to use the Iceman's body for scientific research? Why or why not? Discuss with a partner.

I think we should use the Iceman's body for scientific research because …

I think we should leave the Iceman's body untouched as …

B Look back at your answers to exercise F in Understanding the Reading 1. Based on information in the video, are you more certain or less certain than before about how the Iceman died? Why? Discuss with a partner.

Reading 2

PREPARING TO READ

A The words and phrases in **blue** below are used in Reading 2. Complete the sentences with the correct form of each word or phrase.

Your **identity** is who you are.

If you **obtain** something, you get it.

You can use *moreover* to mean "in addition."

If something is **unclear**, it is not definite or easy to understand.

If you **mention** something, you say something about it.

If you **suffer from** something, you are badly affected by it.

If you **carry out** a job or a task, you do it or finish it.

A **sample** of something is a small amount that shows characteristics of the whole thing.

An **archaeologist** is a person who finds and examines objects from the past.

A **combination** of two or more things is the result of putting those things together.

1. Due to the lack of evidence, the cause of the victim's death is still _____.

2. In his article, the author _____ that he is a(n) _____ and a scholar of ancient history.

3. The _____ of an old wound and a full stomach indicated that the Iceman probably was not in a fight when he was killed.

4. Some researchers think that the Iceman _____ heart disease. This may give us clues about what life was like in ancient times. _____, it may help us understand new ways to help people avoid the disease.

5. Researchers _____ CT scans of the Iceman's body. They also used DNA analysis to _____ information about his mysterious death.

6. The blood in a leech at a crime scene matched a DNA _____ taken from one of the robbers, so police were able to determine his _____.

B Discuss these questions with a partner.

1. What questions about the past do you think **archaeologists** are trying to answer?

2. Why might it be challenging to **obtain** clues or evidence in their research?

C Read the title and the headings in the reading passage. Which two mysteries do you think the passage investigates? Check your answers as you read.

☐ 1. how a pharaoh's tomb was robbed

☐ 2. what caused a pharaoh's death

☐ 3. who a pharaoh's family members were

KING TUT'S FAMILY SECRETS

by Zahi Hawass

🎧 1.04

As an archaeologist and scholar of ancient Egyptian history, I believe that we should honor the ancient dead and let them rest in peace. On the other hand, there are some secrets of the ancient Egyptian pharaohs that we can learn only by studying their mummies. Let me use the example of King Tutankhamun to illustrate what I mean.

UNLOCKING A MYSTERY

When Tutankhamun died about 3,000 years ago, he was secretly buried in a small tomb near what is now the city of Luxor. When archaeologists rediscovered the tomb in 1922, the king's treasures—more than 5,000 artifacts[1]—were still inside. Among the artifacts was the pharaoh's solid gold coffin and a gold mask. There were also 130 staffs, or walking sticks. Mysteriously, an examination of Tutankhamun's mummy revealed a hole in the back of his skull. Also, there were two mummified fetuses[2] in the tomb.

These mummies and artifacts were an extremely important archaeological discovery, but they did not answer many questions about the young pharaoh and his family. Who were his mother and father? Were the two fetuses his unborn children? Could the hole in Tut's head be related to his cause of death? To solve these mysteries required further study and the use of CT scans and DNA analysis.

ANALYZING TUT

In 2005, my colleagues and I carried out CT scans of Tutankhamun's mummy. We showed

[1] An **artifact** is a culturally or historically significant object that is made by a human being.

[2] A **fetus** is an unborn animal or human being in its later stages of development.

Dr. Zahi Hawass—shown preparing Tutankhamun's body for a CT scan—was the leader of the archaeological team investigating the king's family secrets.

Our team also tested Tutankhamun's mummy for evidence of infectious diseases. We found DNA from a parasite[4] called *Plasmodium falciparum*, which meant that Tutankhamun suffered from malaria. Did malaria kill the king? Perhaps. My opinion, however, is that Tutankhamun's health was endangered the moment he was born. To explain what I mean, let me describe our study of Tutankhamun's royal family.

F

TRACING TUT'S FAMILY TREE

Our team obtained and analyzed DNA samples from Tutankhamun and 10 other mummies we believed were members of his royal family. We knew the identities of three members of his family—Amenhotep III as well as Yuya and Tuyu, who were the parents of Amenhotep III's wife. The other seven mummies were unknown. They comprised an adult male, four adult females, and the two fetuses in Tutankhamun's tomb.

G

We first worked to solve the mystery of Tutankhamun's father. Many scholars believed his father was the pharaoh Akhenaten, but the archaeological evidence was unclear. Through a combination of CT scans and a comparison of DNA, our team was able to confirm Amenhotep III and Tiye—one of the unidentified female mummies—as the grandparents of Tutankhamun. Moreover, our study revealed that the unidentified male adult mummy was almost certainly Akhenaten, a son of Amenhotep III and Tiye. This supported the theory that Akhenaten was Tutankhamun's father.

H

What about Tutankhamun's mother? We discovered that the DNA of one of the unidentified female mummies matched that of the young king. To our surprise, her DNA proved that, like Akhenaten, she was a child of Amenhotep III and Tiye. This meant that Akhenaten and his wife were brother and sister—and Tutankhamun was their son.

I

that the hole in Tutankhamun's skull was made during the mummification process. Our study also showed that Tutankhamun died when he was only 19, soon after fracturing his left leg. However, the CT scans alone could not solve the mystery of how the king died, or why he died so young.

In 2008, my colleagues and I decided to analyze samples of Tutankhamun's DNA. Early in the study, our team made some new discoveries: Tutankhamun's left foot was clubbed,[3] and one toe was missing a bone. A condition known as necrosis (tissue death) had destroyed some bones in the foot. The discovery explained why there were so many staffs in Tutankhamun's tomb. Some scholars had argued that the staffs were symbols of power. Our DNA study showed that the king needed the staffs to walk.

E

[3] When a foot is **clubbed**, it is deformed so that the foot is twisted inward and most of the person's weight rests on the heel.

[4] A **parasite** is a small animal or plant that lives on or inside a larger animal or plant.

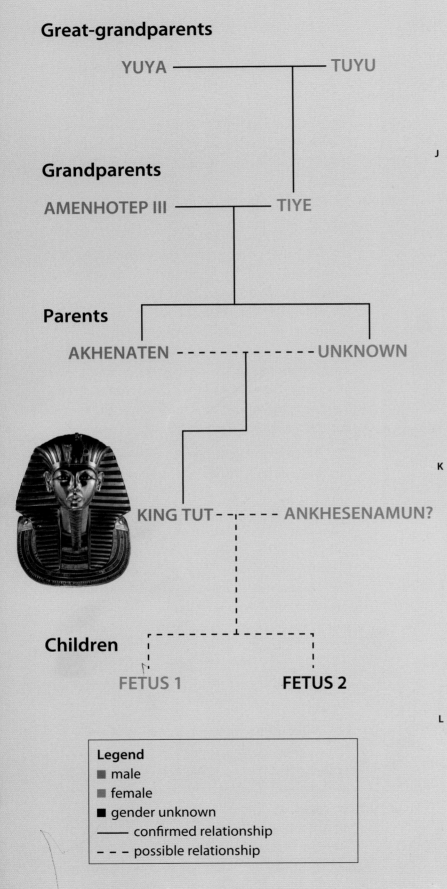

Great-grandparents

YUYA ———————— TUYU

Grandparents

AMENHOTEP III ———— TIYE

Parents

AKHENATEN - - - - - - - UNKNOWN

KING TUT - - - - ANKHESENAMUN?

Children

FETUS 1   FETUS 2

Legend
- ■ male
- ■ female
- ■ gender unknown
- ——— confirmed relationship
- - - - possible relationship

While the data are still incomplete, our study also suggests that one of the mummified fetuses is Tutankhamun's daughter and that the other may also be his child. We have only partial data from the two other unidentified female mummies. One of these may be the mother of the infant mummies and Tutankhamun's wife—possibly a woman named Ankhesenamun. We know from history that she was the daughter of Akhenaten and his wife, Nefertiti, and therefore probably was Tutankhamun's half-sister.

HOW DID TUT DIE?

As I **mentioned** earlier, I believe that Tutankhamun's health was compromised[5] from birth. As our study showed, his mother and father were brother and sister. Such a relationship was common in royal families in ancient Egypt, as it offered political advantages. However, married siblings can pass on harmful genes. Tutankhamun's clubbed foot and bone disease may therefore have been because he had a genetic predisposition.[6] These problems, together with an attack of severe malaria or a broken leg, may have combined to cause the king's premature[7] death.

HONORING THE KING

After Tutankhamun's death, a new dynasty[8] came to power. The rulers of this new dynasty tried to erase all records of Tutankhamun and his royal family from history. Through ongoing DNA research, our team seeks to honor the members of Tutankhamun's family and keep their memories alive.

---

[5] If someone's health is **compromised**, it is weakened.
[6] If you have a **genetic predisposition** to a disease, your DNA makes you more likely to get that disease.
[7] Something that is **premature** happens earlier than people expect.
[8] A **dynasty** is a series of rulers of a country who all belong to the same family.

UNDERSTANDING THE READING

A Write a paragraph letter for each of these main ideas from the reading passage.

UNDERSTANDING
MAIN IDEAS

1. _____5_____ Hawass and his team studied Tut's DNA and found out that he had a bone disease.

2. _____6_____ Tut's health may have been weakened because his parents were siblings.

3. _____1_____ Hawass decided to use technology to answer questions about Tut's life and death.

4. _____4_____ Hawass and his team used DNA samples to determine Tut's father.

5. _____2_____ CT scans provided some information about Tut's body, but didn't show how he died.

6. _____3_____ Hawass's analysis of Tut's DNA revealed that he had suffered from malaria.

B For each statement below, circle T for true, F for false, or NG if the information is not given.

UNDERSTANDING
DETAILS

1. Researchers think the fetuses may have been Tutankhamun's children. **(T)** F NG

2. Tuyu was Tutankhamun's wife. **(T)** F NG

3. Analysis of Tutankhamun's mummy revealed that he was tall. T **(F)** **(NG)**

4. Problems with Tutankhamun's bones and foot may have been genetic health problems. **(T)** F NG

5. Tutankhamun's son became pharaoh after he died. T F **(NG)**

C Put these events (a–g) in the order that they occurred.

SEQUENCING

a. Tutankhamun's tomb was rediscovered.

b. Archaeologists found a hole in Tutankhamun's skull.

c. Hawass and his team made CT scans of Tutankhamun's mummy.

d. Hawass and his team determined the identity of Tutankhamun's father.

e. Hawass and his team decided to study DNA from Tutankhamun's mummy.

f. Hawass and his team studied DNA from one of the female mummies in the tomb.

g. Hawass and his team discovered that Tutankhamun had a clubfoot and bone disease.

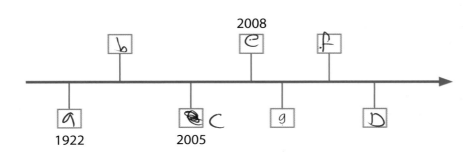

D Find and underline these **bold** words in the reading passage. Use context to identify their meanings. Then write the part of speech and your own definition for each word.

1. **honor** (paragraph A)　　　Part of speech: _noun_

   Meaning: _They are the Scientist who study human bad_

2. **partial** (paragraph J)　　　Part of speech: _Adjective_

   Meaning: _leave Something incomplete_

3. **infant** (paragraph J)　　　Part of speech: _noun_

   Meaning: _A very young body_

4. **siblings** (paragraph K)　　　Part of speech: _noun_

   Meaning: _Childre from same parents or_ _brothers & Sister_

E Look back at the section "Tracing Tut's Family Tree." Find an example of information that is more certain and one that is less certain. Share the reasons for your answers with a partner.

_____

_____

F Work with a partner. Answer the questions below.

1. Based on the information in the text, check (✔) which health issues Hawass thinks may have contributed to Tut's death.

   ☑ 1. a head injury　　　☐ 4. necrosis

   ☑ 2. a broken leg　　　☑ 5. genetic predispositions

   ☑ 3. malaria　　　☑ 6. a clubbed foot

2. Did Hawass and his team solve the mystery of Tut's death? Discuss with a partner.

G Compare Hawass's team's examination of Tutankhamun to scientists' examination of the Iceman. What are some of the similarities and differences? Note your ideas in the diagram. Then share them with a partner.

Examination of Tutankhamun　　　**Examination of the Iceman**

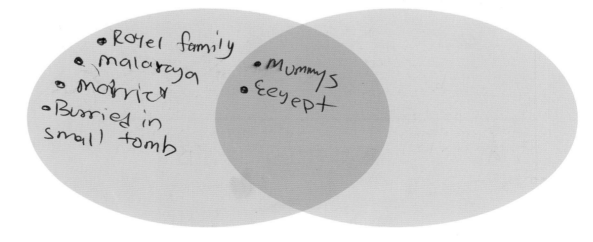

- Royel family
- malaraya
- mothice
- Burried in small tomb
- Mummys
- Eeyept

Writing

EXPLORING WRITTEN ENGLISH

A Read the two paragraphs. What did the writer do to paraphrase the original? Match the changes (a–c) to the highlighted parts.

NOTICING

a. combined two ideas together
b. used a different word with the same meaning
c. used a different part of speech for an idea

Original:

Our team also tested Tutankhamun's mummy for evidence of infectious diseases. We found DNA from a parasite called *Plasmodium falciparum*, which meant that Tutankhamun suffered from malaria. Did malaria kill the king? Perhaps. My opinion, however, is that Tutankhamun's health was endangered the moment he was born. To explain what I mean, let me describe our study of Tutankhamun's royal family.

Paraphrased version:

When Hawass's team examined Tutankhamun's remains for infectious diseases, they discovered from DNA analysis that the king had suffered from malaria. It is therefore possible that Tutankhamun's death was caused by this disease. However, in Hawass's view, Tutankhamun's health was in danger ever since his birth. Hawass describes his team's investigation of the king's royal family to support his opinion.

LANGUAGE FOR WRITING Paraphrasing

When you write a summary, it is important to paraphrase the original; that is, to use your own words to express the same information. Here are three techniques:

1. **Combine ideas.** Use words and phrases such as *and*, *because*, *while*, and *as soon as* to connect ideas. For example, the ideas in the first two sentences in the original paragraph above are combined into one sentence using *When . . . , they . . . .*

2. **Use synonyms.** For example, *investigation* instead of *study* was used in the paraphrased version. It is important to make sure that the synonym matches the context of your sentence. *Learning* is a synonym for *study*, but *investigation* works better in the context of the sentence.

3. **Use different parts of speech.** For instance, the paraphrased example above uses the noun *birth* instead of the adjective *born* to express the same meaning. If the original piece is written in the first person (*I*, *my team*, etc.), you will also need to change the point of view to third person (*He*, *Hawass's team*, etc.).

B Read the sentences and choose the best synonym for each underlined word.

1. After the police questioned him, the suspect eventually <u>admitted</u> to committing the 2001 robbery.

   a. allowed   b. confessed   c. welcomed

2. Scientists guessed that the Iceman might have been resting after a meal when enemies <u>attacked</u> him from behind.

   a. criticized   b. infected   c. assaulted

3. And indeed, a palo verde tree at the scene of the crime looked like a truck might have <u>hit</u> it.

   a. crashed into   b. slapped   c. punched

4. These mummies and artifacts were an extremely important archaeological <u>discovery</u>, but they did not answer many questions about the young pharaoh and his family.

   a. innovation   b. find   c. invention

5. The other seven mummies were <u>unknown</u>.

   a. foreign   b. strange   c. unidentified

6. Such a relationship was common in royal families in ancient Egypt, as it offered political <u>advantages</u>.

   a. improvements   b. benefits   c. pros

C Complete the paraphrased sentences below. Use a different part of speech for the boxed words, and paraphrase the <u>underlined</u> words using suitable synonyms.

1. When most people think of leeches, they imagine disgusting blood-sucking worms that they would prefer to avoid. However, leeches can actually be <u>useful</u>.

   Paraphrase: While most people's _____ is to avoid leeches, they can

   actually be _____ to us.

2. The suspect admitted to giving the victim a ride in his <u>truck</u>, but denied any wrongdoing.

   Paraphrase: The suspect admitted that the victim had _____ in his

   _____, but denied responsibility for the crime.

3. Scientists also discovered a wound on one of his hands. This told them that he had likely been in a fight and that his enemies later chased after and <u>killed</u> him.

   Paraphrase: In addition, the _____ of an injury on one of

   his hands led scientists to believe that he had been in a fight before he was

   _____.

A summary is a short, paraphrased version of an original passage. Paraphrasing is a useful method when writing a summary because you need to report in your own words the most important information in the original passage. Follow these steps to write a summary.

1. Read the passage once. As you read, underline the important facts. Then, without looking at the passage, write notes.

2. Reread the passage, comparing your notes against it to check your understanding. Edit any incorrect notes.

3. Use your notes to write a summary.
   - In a long text, look for sections of an article that discuss the same general idea.
   - Create a topic sentence that expresses the main idea of the section(s) that you are summarizing.
   - Paraphrase important supporting ideas from the original passage.

4. Compare your summary with the original. Make sure that your summary expresses the same meaning as the original, and that the ideas are presented in the same general order. If you use synonyms, check that they are suitable for the context.

5. Check your sentence structures and word choices. If your summary is very similar to the original, combine more ideas and paraphrase using synonyms or different parts of speech.

D Look back at "Researchers Discover Gender-Driven Play in Chimps" in Unit 1, Reading 2. Order the sentences (1–7) to make a summary.

__1__ a. Young primates in captivity often pick out toys based on their gender.

_____ b. Playing with sticks might also just be a way for the chimps to express their imaginations.

_____ c. Young male chimps, on the other hand, play energetically, chasing each other and climbing.

_____ d. Richard Wrangham, a Harvard University primatologist, has recently discovered that Kanyawara chimps in the wild do this, too.

__4__ e. Young female chimps play with sticks and take care of them like dolls or babies.

_____ f. Researchers believe that playing with sticks might have helped female chimps develop mothering skills, which helped their species survive.

_____ g. Young female monkeys choose dolls and young males choose trucks to play with.

WRITING TASK

> **GOAL** You are going to write summaries of two sections of Reading 1 in this unit.

BRAINSTORMING   **A**   Choose two of the sections of Reading 1 below. Without looking back, note down the main ideas of the sections and other important information that you can remember. Then compare the sections with your notes and make any corrections.

- A Robbery Case in Australia
- A Murder Case in Arizona
- A Body in the Mountains

PLANNING   **B**   Follow these steps to make notes for your summaries.

Step 1   Write a topic sentence that expresses the main idea of each section you are going to summarize.

Step 2   For each section, list important ideas that support each topic sentence.

OUTLINE

Summary 1

Topic Sentence: _____

_____

Important Ideas: _____

_____

_____

_____

_____

Summary 2

Topic Sentence: _____

_____

Important Ideas: _____

_____

_____

_____

_____

FIRST DRAFT   **C**   Use the information in your outline to write a first draft of your summaries. Write a paragraph for each one.

REVISING PRACTICE

The drafts below are based on a section of Unit 1, Reading 2.

What did the writer do in Draft 2 to improve the paragraph? Match the changes (a–d) to the highlighted parts.

a. added a topic sentence
b. added a relevant example
c. used a better synonym
d. paraphrased by combining ideas

Draft 1

In elephant groups, females develop lifelong relationships with one another, and help to raise each other's babies. Male elephants also have strong relationships with one another. In male groups, there is a firm hierarchy. Older males act as teachers for younger elephants. They control them when conflict occurs. This organization helps continue the peace when food and water are limited because the young males know that the older ones eat and drink first.

Draft 2

Elephants behave differently in social groups depending on their gender. In elephant groups, females develop lifelong relationships with one another, and help to raise each other's babies. When a baby's mother dies, aunts, grandmothers, and friends act as the orphan's mother. Male elephants also have strong relationships with one another. In male groups, there is a firm hierarchy. Older male elephants teach the younger ones, and have control of them. This organization helps keep the peace when food and water are limited because the young males know that the older ones eat and drink first. ☐ ☐ ☐ ☐

D Now use the questions below to revise each of your summary paragraphs.

REVISED DRAFT

- ☐ Does your topic sentence state the main idea of the section you are summarizing?
- ☐ Did you include all the important information from the section?
- ☐ Did you present the information in the same general order as the original section?
- ☐ Did you paraphrase by combining ideas, using synonyms, or changing the parts of speech where appropriate?

EDITING PRACTICE

Read the information below.

When you use synonyms, make sure your synonym:
- has the same meaning as the original word.
- fits in the context of the sentence.

Correct one mistake with an underlined synonym in each of the paraphrases (1–3). Use a thesaurus to help you.

1. DNA is a <u>tiny</u> molecule containing a code that gives the body <u>instructions</u> for the growth of cells.

   Paraphrase: DNA is a <u>small</u> molecule that contains <u>lessons</u> for a person's cell development.

2. Because each person's DNA is <u>distinctive</u>, it is a <u>valuable</u> tool for identification.

   Paraphrase: Every individual's DNA is <u>diverse</u>, so it is <u>useful</u> in identifying people.

3. Using DNA phenotyping, scientists can <u>determine</u> traits such as a person's eye color, natural hair color, the possible shapes of their facial features, and their geographic <u>ancestry</u>.

   Paraphrase: DNA phenotyping allows scientists to <u>control</u> characteristics such as eye and hair color, facial structure, as well as geographic <u>origin</u>.

FINAL DRAFT   **E**   **Follow these steps to write a final draft.**

1. Check your revised draft for mistakes with using synonyms.
2. Now use the checklist on page 253 to write a final draft. Make any other necessary changes.

UNIT REVIEW

Answer the following questions.

1. How is DNA technology useful in helping detectives solve crimes? Name two ways.

   _____

   _____

   _____

2. What are some ways of paraphrasing information?

   _____

   _____

   _____

3. Do you remember the meanings of these words? Check (✔) the ones you know. Look back at the unit and review the ones you don't know.

   Reading 1:

   ☐ analysis AWL   ☐ commit AWL   ☐ detective AWL
   ☐ determine   ☐ examine   ☐ heal
   ☐ mystery   ☐ prove   ☐ reveal AWL
   ☐ suspect

   Reading 2:

   ☐ archaeologist   ☐ carry out   ☐ combination
   ☐ identity AWL   ☐ mention   ☐ moreover
   ☐ obtain AWL   ☐ sample   ☐ suffer from
   ☐ unclear

CITY SOLUTIONS 3

The bus rapid transit (BRT) network in Curitiba, Brazil, has inspired similar systems in other cities.

THINK AND DISCUSS

1   What are the biggest cities in your country? How would you describe them?
2   What is your favorite city? What do you like about it?

A Look at the information on these pages and answer the questions.

1. What overall trends have occurred in the world's urban population since 1950?

2. Which region had the fastest percentage urban growth from 1950 to 1990? How about from 1990 to 2015?

3. Which regions are projected to urbanize fastest between now and 2050?

B Match the words in yellow to their definitions.

_____ (adj) related to a city

_____ (n) the process of increasing

_____ (adj) having a large number of people and buildings close together

AN URBAN SPECIES

Urban areas of more than a million people were rare until the early 20th century. Today, there are over 30 cities of more than 10 million people. These **dense** areas can have more than 500 inhabitants per square mile (over 195 people per square kilometer).

Growth in these high-density cities is likely to increase even more in the future as populations rise and migration from rural areas continues. In fact, two-thirds of the world's population may live in cities by 2050.

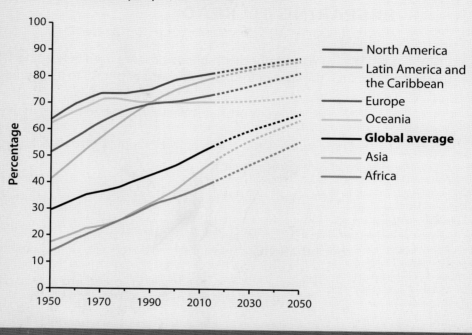

Growing Urbanization

Percentage of population living in urban areas of more than 300,000 people, 1950–2050

Legend:
- North America
- Latin America and the Caribbean
- Europe
- Oceania
- **Global average**
- Asia
- Africa

Y-axis: Percentage (0–100)
X-axis: 1950, 1970, 1990, 2010, 2030, 2050

With a population of about 3 million people, Dubai is the most populous city in the United Arab Emirates.

Reading 1

PREPARING TO READ

BUILDING
VOCABULARY **A** The words and phrases in **blue** below are used in Reading 1. Read the sentences. Then match the correct form of each word or phrase to its definition.

> Houses in the **suburbs** are relatively cheap compared to those in the city center.
>
> Some studies show that employees with flexible working arrangements are happier and more **productive**.
>
> Many governments have policies that support low-**income** families. ˏ
>
> One negative **aspect** of city living is traffic congestion—cities **tend to** have a higher **concentration** of cars on the roads, especially during peak hours.
>
> Major cities such as Tokyo continue to **spread out** as their populations grow.

1. _____ (n) a part or side of something

2. _____ (v) to cover a huge area

3. _____ (n) money that a person earns

4. _____ (adj) able to achieve a significant amount or result

5. _____ (v) to usually do something or be a certain way

6. _____ (n) a huge amount or number of something in one place

7. _____ (n) an area outside of a large city that has homes and businesses

USING
VOCABULARY **B** Discuss these questions with a partner.

1. Would you rather live in a city center, a **suburb**, or a rural area? Why?

2. What **aspects** of city life appeal to you? Which aspects don't you like?

PREDICTING **C** Read the title and the headings in the reading passage. **What do you think the passage is mainly about? Check your idea as you read.**

a. a comparison of large cities in the past and those in the present

b. the environmental challenges that growing cities are facing

c. the positive impacts of urbanization on people and the environment

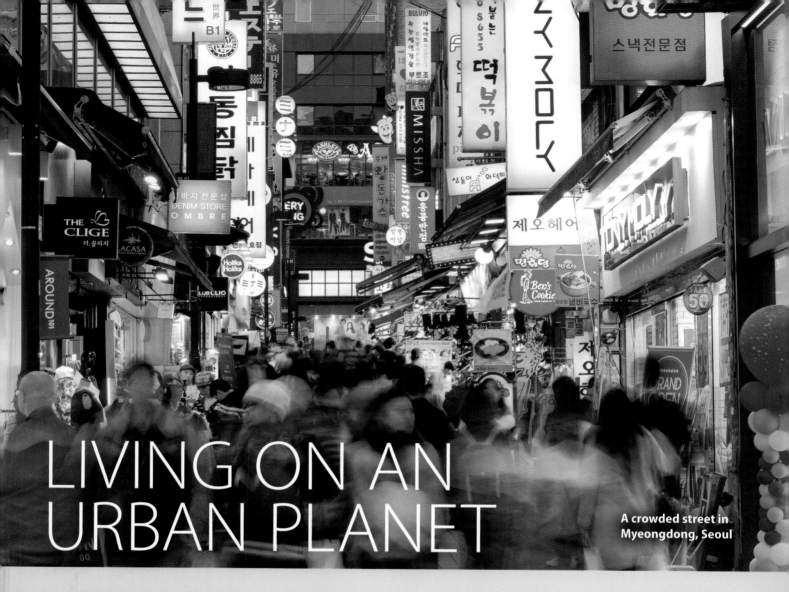

LIVING ON AN URBAN PLANET

A crowded street in Myeongdong, Seoul

🎧 1.05

A   Consider this: in 1800, less than 3 percent of the world's population lived in cities, but by 2050, this could increase to over 66 percent. The trend is clear and the conclusion inescapable—humans have become an urban species.

CITIES AS SOLUTIONS?

B   In the 19th and early 20th centuries, large urban areas began to grow and spread. Many people viewed cities largely in negative terms—crowded, dirty, unhealthy places full of disease and crime. People feared that as cities got bigger, living conditions would get worse. Recent decades, however, have seen a widespread change in attitudes toward urbanization.[1] Many experts believe that urbanization is good news. Although negative aspects such as pollution and urban slums remain serious problems, many urban planners now believe big cities might help solve the problem of Earth's growing population.

[1] **Urbanization** is the process by which cities grow.

The trading floor of the
New York Stock Exchange

Harvard economist Edward Glaeser is one person who believes that cities bring largely positive benefits. According to Glaeser, cities are "the absence of space between people." This closeness reduces the cost of transporting goods, people, and ideas, and allows people to be more productive. Successful cities also attract and reward smart people with higher wages, and they enable people to learn from one another. According to Glaeser, a perfect example of how information can be shared in a big city is the trading floor of the New York Stock Exchange. There, employees share information in one open, crowded space. "They value knowledge over space," he says. "That's what the modern city is all about."

Another champion[2] of urbanization is environmentalist Stewart Brand. According to Brand, living in cities has a smaller impact on the environment than living in suburbs and rural areas. Cities allow half of the world's population to live on about 4 percent of the land. City roads, sewers,[3] and power lines are shorter and require fewer resources to build and operate. City apartments require less energy to heat, cool, and light than houses in other areas. Most

[2] If you are a **champion** of something, you support or defend it.
[3] **Sewers** are large underground channels that carry waste matter and rainwater away.

importantly, Brand points out that people living in dense cities drive less. They can walk to many destinations and use public transportation. As a result, cities tend to produce fewer greenhouse gas emissions per person than suburbs.

Because of these reasons, it may be a mistake to see urbanization as evil. Instead, we should view it as an inevitable part of development, says David Satterthwaite of London's International Institute of Environment and Development. For Satterthwaite and other urban planners, rapid growth itself is not the real problem. The larger issue is how to manage the growth. There is no one model for how to manage rapid urbanization, but there are hopeful examples. One is Seoul, South Korea.

SEOUL'S SUCCESS STORY

Since the 1960s, Seoul's population has increased from fewer than 3 million to more than 10 million people. In the same period, South Korea has also gone from being one of the world's poorest countries to being richer than many countries in Europe. How did this happen? Large numbers of people first began arriving in Seoul in the 1950s. The government soon recognized that economic development was essential for supporting its growing urban population. It therefore began to invest in South Korean companies. This investment eventually helped corporations such as Samsung and Hyundai grow and develop. A major contributing factor for South Korea's economic success was the large number of people who came to Seoul to work.

"You can't understand urbanization in isolation from economic development," says economist Kyung-Hwan Kim of Sogang University. The growing city paid for the buildings, roads, and other infrastructure that helped absorb even more people. South Korea's growth cannot be easily copied. However, it proves that a poor country can urbanize successfully and incredibly fast.

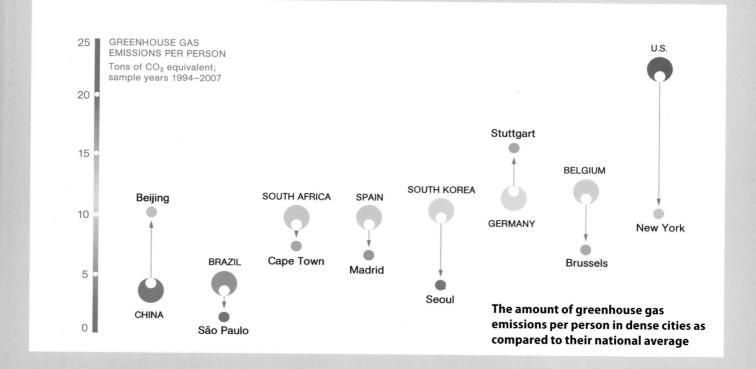

GREENHOUSE GAS
EMISSIONS PER PERSON

Tons of CO_2 equivalent;
sample years 1994–2007

The amount of greenhouse gas emissions per person in dense cities as compared to their national average

MANAGING URBANIZATION

Despite success stories such as Seoul, urban planners around the world continue to struggle with the problem of how to manage urbanization. While they used to worry mainly about city density, urban planners today are focusing on urban sprawl—the way big cities are spreading out and taking over more and more land.

Shlomo Angel is an urban planning professor at New York University and Princeton University. He thinks rising incomes and cheaper transportation are two main reasons for urban sprawl. "When income rises, people have money to buy more space," he says. With cheaper transportation, people can afford to travel longer distances to work. In the second half of the 20th century, for example, many people in the United States moved from cities to suburban areas. This trend led to expanding suburbs, which led to more energy use and increased air pollution and greenhouse gas emissions.

Today, many planners want to bring people back to downtown areas and make suburbs denser. Some ways to densify suburbs include creating walkable town centers, high-rise apartment buildings, and more public transportation. This would make people less dependent on cars. "It would be a lot better for the planet," says Edward Glaeser, if people are "in dense cities built around the elevator rather than in sprawling areas built around the car."

Shlomo Angel believes that planning can make a big difference in the way cities are allowed to grow. However, good planning requires looking decades ahead—reserving land for parks and public transportation, for example, before the city grows over it. It also requires looking at growing cities in a positive way, as concentrations of human energy. With the Earth's population headed toward 9 or 10 billion, dense and carefully planned cities are looking more like a solution—perhaps the best hope for lifting people out of poverty without wrecking[4] the planet.

[4] To **wreck** something means to completely destroy or ruin it.

UNDERSTANDING THE READING

SUMMARIZING **A** Read the first sentence of a summary of "Living on an Urban Planet." Check (✓) four other sentences to complete the summary.

Because most of the world's population will live in cities, it's important to plan and manage cities well so they can benefit society.

☐ 1. Urbanization has a lot of benefits, such as the easy exchange of ideas and the reduction of human impact on the environment.

☐ 2. Seoul experienced many problems as a result of its rapid population growth between 1960 and 2000.

☐ 3. Seoul's successful urbanization is an example of how urbanization can bring positive impacts to cities and countries.

☐ 4. Although some cities have managed to urbanize well, urban planners today are concerned with managing the expansion of large cities.

☐ 5. The second half of the 20th century saw many people in the United States moving out of cities.

☐ 6. Careful long-term planning is key to growing cities that can accommodate the world's future population.

UNDERSTANDING MAIN IDEAS **B** Match each section of the reading passage to its main idea.

_____ 1. Paragraph B   a. Urbanization is better for the environment.

_____ 2. Paragraph C   b. By reducing distance, cities bring largely positive benefits.

_____ 3. Paragraph D   c. Proper urban planning can bring positive results to cities.

_____ 4. Paragraphs F–G   d. Recently, attitudes toward living in cities have become more positive.

_____ 5. Paragraph J

_____ 6. Paragraph K   e. Planners want to reduce the need for cars in suburban areas.

                              f. Well-managed urbanization in the 20th century helped a poor country achieve rapid economic development.

IDENTIFYING PROS AND CONS **C** Answer the questions below with information from the reading passage.

1. According to Edward Glaeser, what are two benefits of living in cities? (paragraph C)

_____

2. According to Stewart Brand, what is one benefit of dense cities? What is one example he gives? (paragraph D)

_____

3. According to David Satterthwaite, what is the main challenge related to urbanization? (paragraph E)

_____

D Read the following quotes from the passage. Which main or supporting idea from the paragraph does each quote support? Discuss with a partner.

1. "They value knowledge over space. That's what the modern city is all about." (paragraph C)

   _____

   _____

2. "You can't understand urbanization in isolation from economic development." (paragraph G)

   _____

   _____

3. "When income rises, people have money to buy more space." (paragraph I)

   _____

   _____

4. "It would be a lot better for the planet [if people are] in dense cities built around the elevator rather than in sprawling areas built around the car." (paragraph J)

   _____

   _____

E Do you think that city life is mainly beneficial? Why or why not? Complete the sentence below. Include at least two reasons. Then share your ideas with a partner.

Overall, I think urbanization has a **positive / negative** impact on human societies because

_____

_____

Shanghai has experienced rapid urbanization since the 1980s.

DEVELOPING READING SKILLS

READING SKILL Analyzing Visual Information

When you first look at a graph, read the title, subtitle, caption, and/or legend (key). Ask yourself what information is being presented. What do the lines, colors, or symbols mean? What is the purpose of the graph? Then underline important words in the title or caption that tell you about the content. Ask yourself how the graph supports the ideas in the reading passage. How does it help you understand the author's ideas better?

ANALYZING VISUAL
INFORMATION

A **Work with a partner. Look at the graph below and answer the questions.**

1. Look at the title, subtitle, and legend. What is the main purpose of the graph?

2. Underline the sentence in the reading passage that the graph relates to.

3. How does the graph support the sentence in the reading passage?

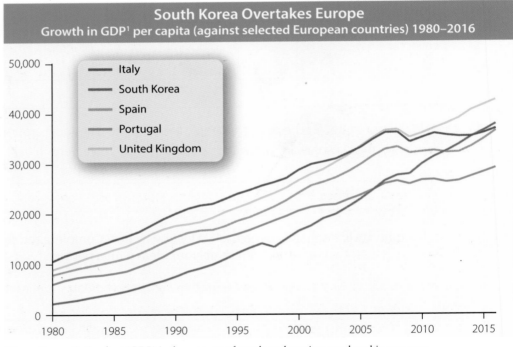

South Korea Overtakes Europe
Growth in GDP[1] per capita (against selected European countries) 1980–2016

Legend:
— Italy
— South Korea
— Spain
— Portugal
— United Kingdom

[1]**Gross Domestic Product** (GDP) is the amount of goods and services produced in one year.

ANALYZING VISUAL
INFORMATION

B **Look at the infographic in the reading passage and answer the questions. Discuss your answers with a partner.**

1. What do the red and green colors indicate? _____ red is down _____

2. What is the main purpose of the chart?

   a. to show the emissions goals of certain cities and countries

   b. to show how some countries have reduced their emissions in the last 25 years

   c. to show how most cities have lower per capita emissions than their countries

3. Which paragraph in the passage does the graph support? _____

Video

FARMING UNDERGROUND

A World War II air raid shelter in London is converted into a farm.

BEFORE VIEWING

A Read the title and the photo caption. Why do you think people would create farms underground? Discuss with a partner.

PREDICTING

B Read the information about food miles—the distance food travels from where it's produced to people's plates—and answer the questions.

LEARNING ABOUT THE TOPIC

How big an impact do "food miles" have on the environment? In some parts of the world, food—such as grains, fruit, and vegetables—travels over 2,400 kilometers to get to consumers. In 2016, the United Kingdom imported about half of its food from other countries. This food is flown or shipped into the country and then transported to towns and cities in trucks. Food transportation trucks produce a quarter of transport-related greenhouse gas emissions—a major cause of global warming. And with an expanding population, these issues are only likely to increase. If producers and consumers are serious about slowing global warming, growing—and buying—more food locally could reduce "food miles."

1. How do "food miles" affect the environment?

   _____

2. Are the problems related to "food miles" likely to increase or decrease in the future? Why?

   _____

3. What do you think is one way to help reduce "food miles" where you live? Note your idea and discuss with a partner.

   _____

C The words and phrases in **bold** below are used in the video. Read the sentences. Then match the correct form of each word or phrase to its definition.

> One way to be more **carbon-neutral** is to drive less and walk more.
>
> **LEDs** save money and energy because they use 90 percent less power than traditional light bulbs.
>
> The **distribution** of food by air and land can cause greenhouse gas emissions.
>
> By **utilizing** new farming technologies—such as **hydroponic farming**—we can use fewer resources to produce the food we need.

1. _____ (n) the act of supplying goods

2. _____ (v) to use something

3. _____ (n) a device that produces light, usually used in electronics

4. _____ (adj) adding no more carbon to the atmosphere than the amount you take in

5. _____ (n) a method of growing plants in mineral-rich water

WHILE VIEWING

A ▶ Watch the video. Check (✓) the reasons Steven Dring and Richard Ballard built an underground farm.

☐ 1. to make young people aware of how food is grown

☐ 2. to grow new types of plants

☐ 3. to cut down on food miles

☐ 4. to help solve environmental problems

☐ 5. to provide food for the growing population of London

☐ 6. to use less water than traditional farming

B ▶ Watch the video again. For each statement below, circle T for true, F for false, or NG if the information is not given.

1. Steven Dring and Richard Ballard built the tunnels.　　　　　　T　F　NG

2. According to Dring, the population in London will increase　　T　F　NG
   by two million in 10 years.

3. The underground farm receives funding from the government.　T　F　NG

4. Dring and Ballard want to grow more plants in the future.　　T　F　NG

AFTER VIEWING

A Steven Dring says, "We've still got kids in the U.K. who think that spaghetti is grown on trees." Why is this a problem? How can the underground farm help solve it? Discuss with a partner.

B What challenges do you think underground farms in cities might face? Think of two ideas. Then share them with a partner.

Reading 2

PREPARING TO READ

BUILDING VOCABULARY

A The words in **blue** below are used in Reading 2. Complete the sentences with the correct words. Use a dictionary to help you.

attempt	basically	consumption	enhance
increasingly	industrial	majority	safety
phenomenon	varied		

1. One way to improve the __Safety__ of city neighborhoods is to have regular police patrols.

2. According to Stewart Brand, city living actually reduces energy __Consumption__ because the __Majority__ of people have access to public transportation and don't have to drive so much.

3. The __Phenomenon__ of urbanization is becoming __increasingly__ common as more and more cities continue to grow and develop.

4. Manchester used to be a(n) __industrial__ city; from cotton to chemicals, there was a(n) __varied__ group of factories and businesses there.

5. Economist Edward Glaeser __basically__ sees cities as places where there is an absence of space between people.

6. The __attempt__ to clean up a small river in downtown Seoul was a success—it helped __enhance__ the attractiveness of the area.

USING VOCABULARY

B Discuss these questions with a partner.

1. What are two ways to **enhance** the quality of life in cities?

2. What can you do to reduce your energy **consumption**?

PREDICTING

C Reading 2 is an interview with Richard Wurman, an urban planner. Wurman studied various cities to learn more about the effects of global urbanization.

What kinds of information about the cities do you think he collected? Discuss with a partner. Then check your ideas as you read.

_____

_____

THE URBAN VISIONARY

🎧 1.06

When architect and urban planner Richard Wurman learned that the **majority** of Earth's population lived in cities, he became curious. He wondered what the effects of global urbanization will be. With a group of business and media partners, Wurman set out on a five-year study—a project called 19.20.21—to collect information about urbanization, focusing on the world's largest urban concentrations, or megacities.

The project's aim is to standardize the way information about cities—such as health, education, transportation, energy **consumption**, and arts and culture—is collected and shared. The hope is that urban planners will be able to use these objective data to **enhance** the quality of life for people in cities while reducing the environmental impact of urbanization.

Q: What draws people to cities?

Wurman: People flock to cities because of the possibilities for doing things that interest them. Those interests—and the economics that make them possible—are based on people living together. We really have turned into a world of cities. Cities cooperate with each other. Cities trade with each other. Cities are where you put museums, where you put universities, where you put the centers of government, the centers of corporations. The inventions, the discoveries, the music and art in our world all take place in these intense gatherings of individuals.

Q: Tell us about 19.20.21.

Wurman: For the first time in history, more people live in cities than outside them. I thought I'd try to discover what this new **phenomenon** really means. I went to the Web, and I tried to find the appropriate books and lists that would give me information, data, maps, so I could

❝One has to understand [a city's problems] in context and in comparison to other places.❞

understand. And I couldn't find what I was looking for. I couldn't find maps of cities to the same scale. Much of the statistical information is gathered independently by each city, and the questions they ask are often not the same. There's no readily available information on the speed of growth of cities. Diagrams on power, water distribution and quality, health care, and education aren't available, so a metropolis[1] can't find out any information about itself relative to other cities and, therefore, can't judge the success or failure of programs.

[1] A **metropolis** is a large, important, busy city.

So I decided to gather consistent information on 19 cities that will have more than 20 million people in the 21st century. That's what 19.20.21 is about. We'll have a **varied** group of young cities, old cities, third-world cities, second-world cities, first-world cities, fast-growing cities, slow-growing cities, coastal cities, inland cities, **industrial** cities, [and] cultural cities. Much of this can be presented online, but we're also planning to have exhibits and urban observatories so that cities around the world can see themselves relative to others.

Q: What are some of the cities you're looking at?

Wurman: What inspires me is being able to understand something, and understanding often comes from looking at extremes. So the cities that pop out are the ones that are clearly the largest, the oldest, the fastest-growing, the lowest, the highest, the densest, the least dense, [or] the largest in area. The densest city is Mumbai. The fastest-growing is Lagos.[2] For years, the largest city was Mexico City, but Tokyo is now the biggest … There are cities that are **basically** spread out, like Los Angeles. Then there are classic cities, which you certainly wouldn't want to leave out, like Paris. I find the data on cities to be endlessly fascinating. Just look at the world's 10 largest cities through time. The biggest city in the year 1000 was Córdoba, Spain. Beijing was the biggest city in 1500 and 1800, London in 1900, New York City in 1950, and today [it's] Tokyo.

[2]In 2017, Dhaka was the densest city, and Zinder was the fastest-growing.

Today, Plaza de la Corredera in Córdoba is a popular place for visitors to the city.

Q: Cities are increasingly challenged to sustain their infrastructure and service. Can they survive as they are now?

Wurman: Nothing survives as it is now. All cities are cities for the moment, and our thoughts about how to make them better are thoughts at the moment. There was great passion 30 years ago for the urban bulldozer,[3] that we had to tear down the slums, tear down the old parts of cities, and have urban renewal. That lasted for about 10, 15 years, until it didn't seem to work very well. And yet the reasons for doing it seemed justified at that moment … It shows that the attempt to make things better often makes things worse. We have to understand before we act. And although there are a lot of little ideas for making things better—better learning, increased safety, cleaner air—you can't solve the problem with a collection of little ideas. One has to understand them in context and in comparison to other places.

[3] A **bulldozer** is a large vehicle used for knocking down buildings.

THE URBAN OBSERVATORY

Wurman's team has created an interactive online exhibit called the Urban Observatory. Hoping to make the world's data "understandable and useful," the website has maps that compare different cities according to a variety of themes. These themes include the types of occupations people have, the types of transportation available, and the quality of public spaces, such as parks.

▲ The maps above show the distribution of green spaces in three major cities.

UNDERSTANDING THE READING

A Choose the best alternative title for the reading passage.

a. An Idea for Sharing Urban Data

b. An Idea for Improving Urban Areas

c. An Idea for Controlling Urban Expansion

UNDERSTANDING
MAIN IDEAS

B Match each section in the passage to its purpose.

_____ 1. Paragraph B

_____ 2. Paragraph C

_____ 3. Paragraph D

_____ 4. Paragraphs E–F

_____ 5. Paragraph G

a. to state what the project wants to achieve

b. to give reasons why more people are moving to cities

c. to give advice on how cities should manage their development

d. to describe the types of data included in the project and what they show

e. to explain the challenges Wurman faced when studying urbanization

UNDERSTANDING
PURPOSE

C Complete the concept map using information from paragraphs A, B, D, and E. Write no more than two words or a number in each space.

UNDERSTANDING
DETAILS

Origins

- created by Richard Wurman, an [1]_____ and urban planner

- Wurman was curious how [2]_____ will change the world

- he set up 19.20.21 with a team of people working in [3]_____ and [4]_____

- the project was expected to last for [5]_____

Aims

- to [6]_____ the collection of city data so that it's easier to compare, e.g., all city maps use the same scale

- the data can then be used by [7]_____ to improve city living

- Wurman hopes urbanization can then have a more positive [8]_____

19.20.21

Methods

- data is collected from the world's largest cities

- study focuses on cities with populations of over [9]_____ people

- looks at how people use transportation, how much [10]_____ they consume, etc.

- information will be shared [11]_____ and via exhibits and other events

D Find the following words and phrases in the reading passage. Use context to identify their meanings. Then circle the best option to complete the definitions.

> draw (paragraph C)   pop out (paragraph F)
>
> flock (paragraph C)   slum (paragraph G)
>
> relative to (paragraph D)

1. Things that *draw* people to a city make them want to **go there / stay away**.

2. When people *flock* to a place, they go in **small / large** numbers.

3. *Relative to* something means **in comparison with / connected to** it.

4. If information *pops out*, you notice it more because it is **detailed / obvious**.

5. *Slums* are parts of cities where living conditions are very **poor / good**.

E Look at the maps in the reading passage and answer the questions below.

1. What do the maps show?

   _____

2. Which city has the greatest amount? Which has the least?

   _____

3. How might this information be useful for cities?

   _____

   _____

F Read the statements below. Which of the people in this unit—Glaeser, Brand, Angel, or Wurman—would agree most strongly with each one? Write a name for each statement. More than one answer is possible. Then share your answers with a partner.

1. Overall, people living in cities have a smaller carbon footprint.   _____

2. It's better to make decisions about a city after looking at it alongside others.   _____

3. Cities are efficient and important places for people to share ideas and information. _____

4. Proper planning is the way to manage urban growth and overcome problems.   _____

Writing

EXPLORING WRITTEN ENGLISH

A Read the sentences (a–c) and notice the underlined verbs. Match each sentence to the most suitable description. NOTICING

   a. In 2017, Steven Dring and Richard Ballard <u>set up</u> an underground farm in London.

   b. Richard Wurman's team <u>has created</u> an online exhibit for the Urban Observatory.

   c. Edward Glaeser <u>has written</u> a number of books about cities.

   _____ 1. The action happened at an unspecified time in the past.

   _____ 2. The action happened several times in the past.

   _____ 3. The action happened at a specific time in the past.

LANGUAGE FOR WRITING Using the Simple Past and the Present Perfect

We use the simple past to describe actions that began and ended in the past.

   *The Highline—a green space in New York City—**opened** to the public in 2009.*

We use the present perfect tense to talk about:

1. something that happened several times in the past.

   *Planners **have redeveloped** this area three times.*

2. something that happened at an unspecified time in the past.

   *The Urban Observatory **has gathered** data from many different cities.*

Note: To form the present perfect, use *have* or *has* and the past participle of a main verb.

B Circle the correct options to complete the sentences.

   1. Large numbers of people **moved** / **have moved** to Seoul during the 1950s.

   2. In the 1950s, the South Korean government **invested** / **has invested** in local companies such as Samsung and Hyundai in order to support the country's economic growth.

   3. Before the 20th century, South Korea **was** / **has been** one of the world's poorest countries.

   4. Overall, life **improved** / **has improved** for South Koreans during the past few decades.

   5. In 1961, the life expectancy in South Korea was 51 years. Since then, it **increased** / **has increased** to 79 years.

WRITING SKILL Writing an Introductory Paragraph

The first paragraph of an essay is the **introductory paragraph**. This paragraph contains the thesis statement and general information about the essay. It can also include a **hook**—an opening sentence to make the reader interested. The hook can be a surprising fact, an interesting question, or an imaginary situation related to the topic. See the first sentence of paragraph A, Reading 1, for an example.

A **thesis statement** is usually the last sentence in the introductory paragraph. It expresses the main idea of an entire essay. Here's an example of a thesis statement for a problem-solution essay:

With more convenient public transportation and pedestrian-only streets, Morristown is now an environmentally friendly and healthy place for its residents.

A good thesis statement gives the writer's position about the topic and states the main points of the essay.

Note: In an introduction, you should avoid using *I* unless you are writing a personal essay. For example, you should avoid saying *I am going to write about . . . .*

C Read the following pairs of thesis statements. Choose the one in each pair that you think is better. Share the reasons for your answers with a partner.

1. a. Life is a lot better in Philadelphia than it was a few years ago for several good reasons.
   b. Life is a lot better in Philadelphia today because there is less crime and more job opportunities.

2. a. Two recent changes have improved the city of San Pedro: new streetlights and better roads.
   b. Most residents of San Pedro are very pleased with the recent infrastructure improvements.

D Choose the best opening hook for each essay topic. Then discuss with a partner.

1. **Topic:** making parking in the city center more convenient
   a. I used to avoid going downtown because it always took me a really long time to find parking.
   b. How long is too long to look for parking downtown? Ten minutes? Fifteen minutes? An hour?

2. **Topic:** improving road safety in cities
   a. Each year, more than 800 people are hit by cars in San Francisco.
   b. A lot of people get hit by cars in San Francisco while they're trying to cross the street.

3. **Topic:** managing traffic congestion in cities
   a. Traffic is terrible in my city because there are too many cars on the road and as a result, it takes a really long time to get anywhere.
   b. Imagine this: It's 8 a.m. You have 30 minutes to get to your job on the other side of town. The traffic is terrible—you'll never make it.

E Match the topics in exercise D to their thesis statements below. One statement is extra.

_____ a. With the introduction of a new subway line and increased housing in the city, there should now be fewer cars on the roads during peak hours.

_____ b. In response to the problem, the government has set stricter rules on where you can leave your car in the city center.

_____ c. To ensure the well-being of all road users, city planners have now put more stoplights and created more areas where cars can't go.

_____ d. The increased number of garages in the central district has made it easier for drivers to find a space to leave their cars when they visit.

WRITING SKILL Writing a Concluding Paragraph

The last paragraph of an essay is the **concluding paragraph**. This paragraph usually includes a **summary statement** and sometimes leaves the reader with a **final thought** about the topic. The summary statement paraphrases the thesis statement. Notice in the summary statement below how the author restates the thesis statement in the Writing Skill box in different words.

> _Improved public transportation and pedestrian-only streets have given Morristown cleaner air and a more sustainable future._

Here are two ways to leave the reader with a final thought.

- Make a prediction: _The effects of these improvements to life in Morristown may encourage more people to move here._

- Ask a question: _Will these improvements inspire city officials to make even more environmentally friendly changes in Morristown?_

F Write a summary statement for each thesis statement in exercise E.

_____

_____

_____

_____

_____

_____

G Choose one of the summary statements in exercise F and write a final thought.

_____

_____

WRITING TASK

> **GOAL** You are going to write a problem-solution essay on the following topic:
> Describe a problem that a city or town had, and explain one thing that was done to solve it.

BRAINSTORMING **A** Think of a city or town that is better to live in now than it used to be. Make a list of improvements that were made. Think about areas such as housing, environmental issues, traffic, public transportation, and job opportunities. Do research if necessary.

PLANNING **B** Follow these steps to make notes for your essay.

Step 1 Choose the problem that you want to write about. Note it in the outline, and note two effects of the problem as your supporting ideas.

Step 2 Describe the best solution to the problem. Note two ways it helped solve the problem.

Step 3 Write a thesis statement that states the problem and the solution. Add a hook to your introduction.

Step 4 Write a summary statement and add a final thought for the concluding paragraph.

OUTLINE

Introductory Paragraph

Hook: _____

Thesis Statement: _____

_____

The Problem: _____

Supporting Idea 1 / Details: _____

_____

Supporting Idea 2 / Details: _____

_____

The Solution: _____

Supporting Idea 1 / Details: _____

_____

Supporting Idea 2 / Details: _____

_____

Concluding Paragraph

Summary Statement: _____

Final Thought: _____

REVISING PRACTICE

The draft below is similar to the one you are going to write. Follow the steps to create a better second draft.

1. Add the sentences (a–c) in the most suitable spaces.
   a. It was dirty and dark, with a lot of noise from the cars rushing overhead.
   b. What other improvements might make the city an even more beautiful place to live and visit?
   c. Imagine your shock when you visit San Francisco for the first time, and you have to walk under an ugly freeway to get to the bay.

2. Now fix the following problems (d–f) in the essay.
   d. Cross out one sentence that does not relate to the topic sentence in paragraph B.
   e. Correct a mistake with the simple past or present perfect in paragraph B.
   f. Correct a mistake with the simple past or present perfect in paragraph C.

A

_____ It isn't what you expected. Parts of the city are actually unattractive. However, one improvement that has made the city a more beautiful place for residents and tourists is tearing down the Embarcadero freeway.

B

For three decades until the early 1990s, the Embarcadero freeway was one of the least attractive parts of San Francisco. The two-level freeway completely blocked the view of the bay and sites in the bay, such as Angel Island and Alcatraz. Visitors can take ferries to Alcatraz and take a tour of the old prison. In addition, pedestrians had to walk underneath this 150,000-ton cement structure in order to get from downtown to the bay. Walking under the freeway has not been a pleasant experience. _____

C

In 1989, part of the freeway has been destroyed by an earthquake; two years later, the city authorities decided to take the whole thing down and renovate the area. One way that this has helped make San Francisco more beautiful is by giving people access to the bay. People are able to walk or jog along the Embarcadero or just enjoy views of the Bay Bridge, the water, and the hills and neighboring cities on the other side of the bay. Tearing down the freeway has also allowed residents and tourists to see the beautiful Ferry Building, one of San Francisco's most important buildings. The Ferry Building was closed for decades, but since the renovation, it has been open, and now houses great shops and restaurants. The once ugly Embarcadero has become a place that residents and tourists want to visit.

D

The removal of the Embarcadero freeway has made the waterfront area attractive and accessible for both visitors and San Franciscans. Today, most people don't even remember the old freeway. _____

D Now use the questions below to revise your essay.

☐ Does your introductory paragraph have an interesting hook and a clear thesis statement?

☐ Did you include enough details to explain the problem and the solution in your body paragraphs?

☐ Does your concluding paragraph have a summary statement and a final thought?

EDITING PRACTICE

Read the information below.

In sentences using the present perfect, remember to:
- use the correct form of *have*.
- use the correct form of the past participle of the main verb.

Correct one mistake with the present perfect in each of the sentences (1–5).

1. The city have made a lot of changes over the past 10 years.

2. Residents have enjoy the renovations to the city center and the public parks.

3. The new subway system has make it easier to get across town.

4. It is now safer for people to ride their bikes to work because the government has add bicycle lanes to busy streets.

5. San Francisco city planners has created a beautiful walkable area alongside the bay.

E Follow these steps to write a final draft.

1. Check your revised draft for mistakes with the simple past and the present perfect.

2. Now use the checklist on page 253 to write a final draft. Make any other necessary changes.

UNIT REVIEW
Answer the following questions.

1. Why might living in cities be better than living in the suburbs? List two reasons.

_____

_____

_____

2. What should you include in a thesis statement?

_____

_____

_____

3. Do you remember the meanings of these words? Check (✔) the ones you know. Look back at the unit and review the ones you don't know.

Reading 1:

☐ aspect AWL ☐ concentration AWL ☐ dense

☐ growth ☐ income AWL ☐ productive

☐ spread out ☐ suburb ☐ tend to

☐ urban

Reading 2:

☐ attempt ☐ basically ☐ consumption AWL

☐ enhance AWL ☐ increasingly ☐ industrial

☐ majority AWL ☐ phenomenon AWL ☐ safety

☐ varied AWL

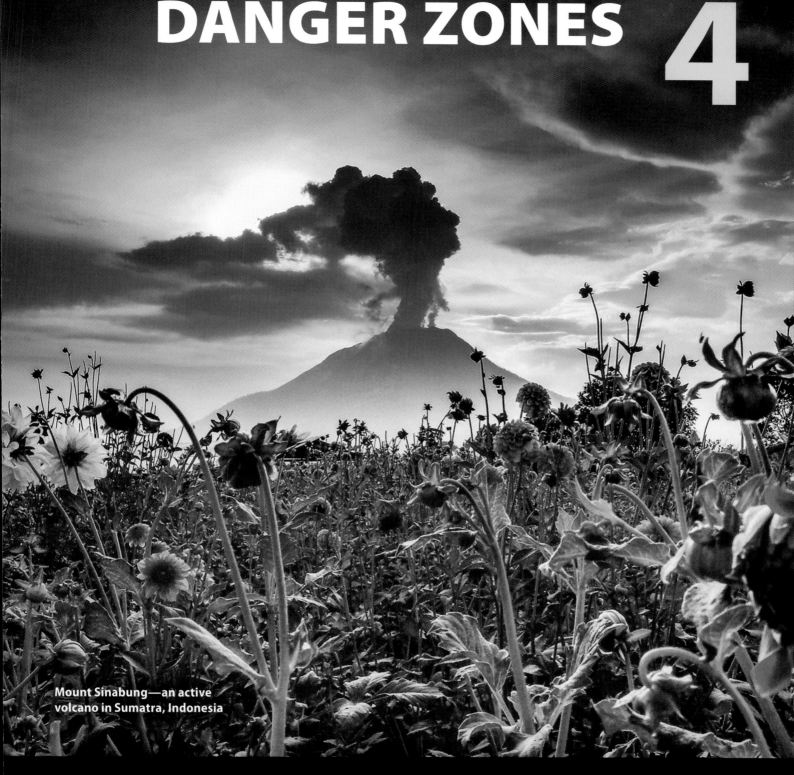

DANGER ZONES

Mount Sinabung—an active volcano in Sumatra, Indonesia

ACADEMIC SKILLS

READING	Understanding referencing and cohesion
WRITING	Writing a process essay
GRAMMAR	Using parallel structures
CRITICAL THINKING	Inferring

THINK AND DISCUSS

1 What extreme natural events can be dangerous to humans?

2 Why do you think some people live in areas that are affected by extreme natural events?

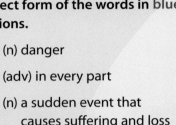

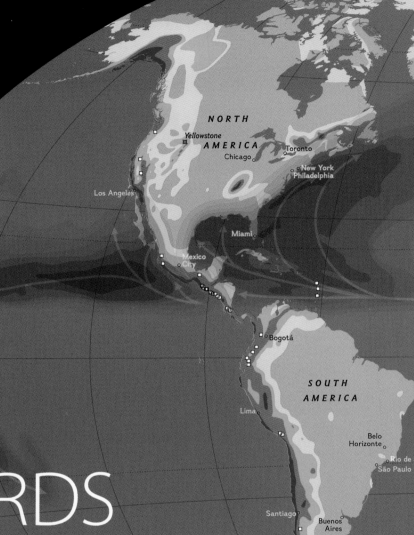

A Look at the information on these pages and answer the questions.

1. Where in the world do most of the following occur?
   - earthquakes
   - volcanoes
   - cyclones

2. What do many of the places affected by natural hazards have in common?

B Match the correct form of the words in blue to their definitions.

_____ (n) danger

_____ (adv) in every part

_____ (n) a sudden event that causes suffering and loss

NORTH
AMERICA

Yellowstone
Chicago
Toronto
New York
Philadelphia
Los Angeles
Miami
Mexico City
Bogotá

SOUTH
AMERICA

Lima
Belo Horizonte
Rio de Janeir
São Paulo
Santiago
Buenos Aires

WORLD
OF HAZARDS

Natural **hazards** occur **throughout** the world, but mostly happen in certain vulnerable areas. For example, most earthquakes and volcanoes occur at or near plate boundaries. Large storm systems (known as cyclones in the Indian Ocean, hurricanes in the Atlantic, and typhoons in the Pacific) form in the tropics and cause serious coastal flooding.

Unfortunately, as the map shows, many of the world's most highly populated areas are also the most hazardous. With more people, the cost of natural hazards is significant. In 2016, natural **disasters** in Asia resulted in over 80 billion dollars in damage cost.

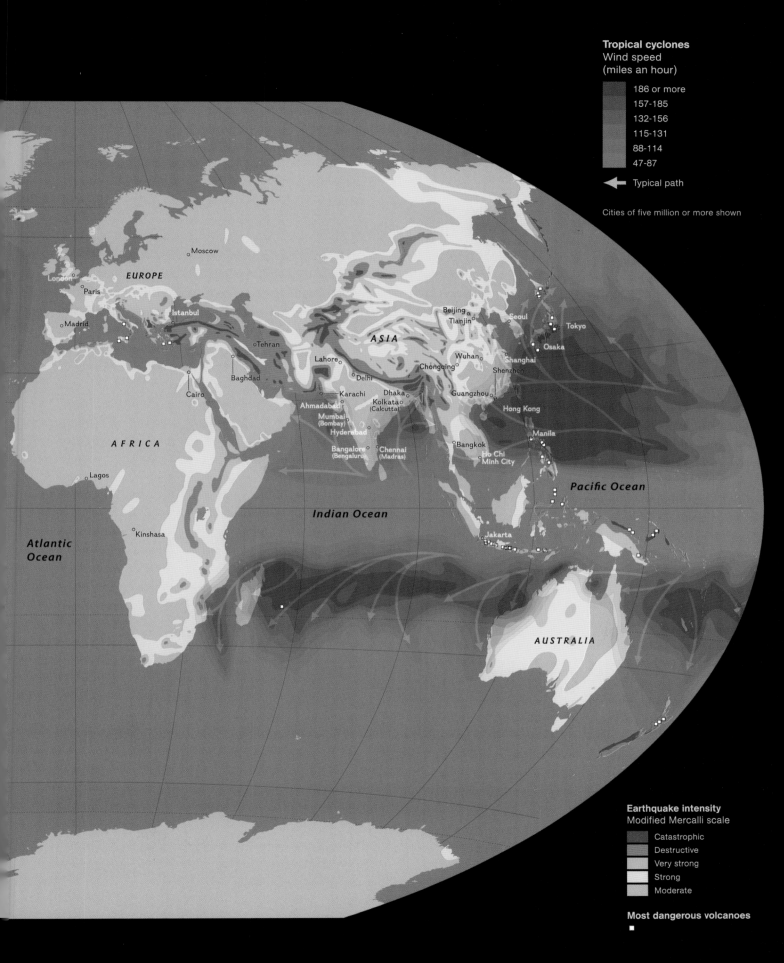

Tropical cyclones
Wind speed
(miles an hour)

186 or more
157-185
132-156
115-131
88-114
47-87

⬅ Typical path

Cities of five million or more shown

Moscow

EUROPE

London
Paris

Istanbul

Madrid

Tehran

Baghdad

Cairo

Lahore

ASIA

Delhi

Beijing
Tianjin

Seoul

Tokyo

Osaka

Wuhan

Shanghai

Chongqing

Shenzhen

AFRICA

Karachi

Ahmadabad
Mumbai
(Bombay)
Hyderabad

Dhaka

Kolkata
(Calcutta)

Guangzhou

Hong Kong

Manila

Bangalore
(Bengaluru)

Chennai
(Madras)

Bangkok

Lagos

Ho Chi
Minh City

Pacific Ocean

Kinshasa

Indian Ocean

Jakarta

Atlantic
Ocean

AUSTRALIA

Earthquake intensity
Modified Mercalli scale

Catastrophic
Destructive
Very strong
Strong
Moderate

Most dangerous volcanoes
■

Reading 1

PREPARING TO READ

BUILDING VOCABULARY

A The words and phrases in blue below are used in Reading 1. Read the paragraph. Then match the correct form of each word or phrase to its definition.

Every year, **deadly** earthquakes kill thousands of people and cause massive **destruction** to buildings. A system that **forecasts** when a natural disaster is about to occur and **alerts** people would potentially save many lives. With enough warning, people could **get out** of the area and avoid the disaster. Scientists and researchers are trying to develop systems like this, but the process can be expensive and the systems don't work **effectively** all of the time. Hopefully, one day, **affordable** and accurate early-warning systems will save lives in vulnerable places around the world.

1. _____ (v) to warn

2. _____ (v) to predict

3. _____ (n) severe damage

4. _____ (v) to leave; to escape

5. _____ (adj) not too expensive

6. _____ (adv) in a way that works well

7. _____ (adj) so dangerous that it can cause death

USING VOCABULARY

B Discuss these questions with a partner.

1. What kinds of natural **disasters** occur in your country?

2. How do officials in your country **alert** people when a natural **hazard** might occur?

BRAINSTORMING

C What are two ways in which scientists predict natural hazards such as earthquakes and tornadoes? Discuss with a partner.

PREDICTING

D Skim the first two paragraphs of the reading passage. How do you think animals might sense danger? Note two ways. Then check your ideas as you read.

_____

_____

Scientists think that some bird species can sense when danger is approaching.

SENSING DISASTER

🎧 1.07

A   Twenty-three hundred years ago, hordes[1] of mice, snakes, and insects fled the Greek city of Helike on the Gulf of Corinth. "After these creatures departed, an earthquake occurred in the night," wrote the ancient Roman writer Claudius Aelianus. "The city subsided;[2] an immense wave flooded and Helike disappeared."

B   Scientists have long suspected that animals might have a "sixth sense." This sense alerts them when natural hazards—like earthquakes and tornadoes—are about to strike. Until recently, though, we have had to rely on informal reports of changes in animal behavior. However, scientists have now begun to detect evidence that suggests animals can indeed make predictions.

---

[1] **Hordes** are large moving groups.
[2] To **subside** is to go down to a lower or the normal level.

A tapir captured by a motion-triggered camera in Panama

A NATURAL WARNING

In 2011, a research team began a study of animal behavior in Yanachaga National Park in the Peruvian Amazon. In order to track animal movements, the team placed motion-triggered cameras **throughout** the park. On a single day, the cameras typically recorded up to 15 animal sightings.[3] Then the researchers noticed a change: Over a three-week period, the sightings dropped to fewer than five a day. In the last few days, there were no animal sightings at all.

The researchers were puzzled: this was highly unusual behavior, especially in a rain forest area normally filled with wildlife. But then, at the end of the three-week period, disaster struck. On August 24, the area was hit by a 7.0 magnitude earthquake. Could the animals have left the area—or found places to hide—because they sensed the earthquake was coming?

"As far as we know, this is the first time that motion-triggered cameras have documented this phenomenon prior to an earthquake," says lead researcher Dr. Rachel Grant. She believes the findings could have important consequences for earthquake prediction. "Animals have the potential to be reliable forecasters of earthquakes and could be used alongside other monitoring systems," she says. Cameras that track animal movements could therefore be used as an **affordable** early warning system.

Scientists are not certain why animal movements might change before earthquakes. However, Grant has a theory. Prior to an earthquake, large forces stress the Earth's surface and change the atmosphere. The atmospheric changes can, in turn, cause increased serotonin[4] levels in animals and humans, leading to unpleasant feelings of restlessness.[5] Two weeks before the earthquake

---

[3] **Sightings** are occasions in which something is observed.

[4] **Serotonin** is a chemical in the body that affects the sleep-wake cycle.
[5] **Restlessness** is a state of not being able to relax.

in Peru, a significant atmospheric change was recorded. Eight days before the quake, it became even more intense, possibly causing the animals to leave the area.

When it comes to predicting earthquakes, rodents such as rats appear to be the most sensitive animals in the rain forest. "What was interesting was that rodents were the first to disappear," Grant says. "They were nowhere to be seen eight days before the earthquake … That they should completely disappear was amazing." Grant believes that recent research in China and Japan may help explain why this happened. According to these studies, rats' sleeping and waking patterns are disturbed in the days leading up to an earthquake. These changes may alert them to a coming disaster.

FOLLOW THE BIRDS

Like rats, birds may also be sensitive to subtle changes in the environment. In fact, scientists have recently learned that some birds may be able to sense severe storms before they arrive.

In 2014, a team of U.S. scientists studied the migration patterns of golden-winged warblers. To track the birds' movements, the researchers attached small, lightweight geolocators that recorded the birds' locations. In April, the team expected to find the warblers in the Cumberland Mountains of eastern Tennessee, where they breed and raise their young. But the birds were not there. Instead, they discovered that most of the birds had flown to Florida; one had even traveled to Cuba.

Several days later, the birds arrived back in Tennessee—after a mysterious round-trip journey of more than 900 miles (1,500 kilometers). The researchers finally worked out what may have prompted the trip. At around the time the birds left Tennessee, a severe weather system was approaching the Midwest region. The deadly storms created more than 80 tornadoes and left at least 35 people dead.

Scientists theorize the warblers were alerted by infrasound—a type of low-frequency noise—produced by the storms. Humans can't hear infrasound, but birds can. It appears the warblers detected the weather system and decided to get out of the way. "We were completely blown away by this behavior," says researcher Gunnar Kramer, a population ecologist at the University of Minnesota. "It shows that the birds can do more than we give them credit for."

Eventually, scientists hope that signs from the natural world might help us forecast earthquakes and serious weather events more effectively. Even a few minutes' warning could be enough for people to avoid the destruction that severe storms and earthquakes can cause. Over two thousand years ago, it seems the animals in Helike had an important message to share. It's only now that we're really paying attention.

A golden-winged warbler

UNDERSTANDING THE READING

SUMMARIZING **A** Complete the summary of the passage using suitable words. Write one word in each space.

Scientists think that animals might be able to [1] _____Sense_____ some natural hazards. By studying their [2] _____behavior_____, scientists have observed that animals seem to be sensitive to small [3] _Movement_ in the atmosphere in the days before the hazard strikes. For example, in one study, animals were observed leaving just before a(n) [4] _deadly Storms_. In another study, birds left an area just before a destructive [5] _earthquick_ arrived.

UNDERSTANDING A PROCESS **B** How do researchers think animals sense earthquakes? Put the events (a–e) in order.

a. animals leave the area
b. serotonin levels in animals rise
c. forces stress the surface of Earth
d. animals become restless
e. Earth's atmosphere changes

Several days before the earthquake:

UNDERSTANDING MAIN IDEAS **C** Use the information from the section "Follow the Birds" to answer the questions.

1. What was the purpose of the geolocators?
   Change of environment
   To to know If they can understand
   To know the bird location

2. Why were the researchers surprised to find the warblers in Florida and Cuba?
   deadly Storms came

3. What probably caused the birds to leave Tennessee?
   To be safe from deadly storms

4. Why does Kramer say "birds can do more than we give them credit for"?
   Because they are smarter then US.
   ad sense stuff

UNDERSTANDING DETAILS **D** Read the statements about the section "A Natural Warning." For each statement, circle T for true, F for false, or NG if the information is not given.

1. In the three-week period before a 7.0 earthquake in Peru, there were more animal sightings than usual. **T** F NG

2. According to Grant, this is the first time that motion-triggered cameras have recorded animals leaving an area before an earthquake. **T** F NG

3. There was a change in the atmosphere two weeks before the earthquake in Peru. T **F** **NG**

4. Serotonin levels in people are not affected by changes in the atmosphere. T F **NG**

5. The research in China and Japan was part of a wider study that observed the behavior of several animal species. **T** F NG

E Find and underline the following **bold** words and phrases in the passage. Use context to identify their meanings. Then match the sentence parts to form definitions. INFERRING MEANING

_d_ 1. Paragraph E: If someone has **documented** something,

_e_ 2. Paragraph H : If you are **sensitive** to the surrounding environment,

_c_ 3. Paragraph H: If something is **subtle**,

_a_ 4. Paragraph J: When someone **prompts** you to do something,

_b_ 5. Paragraph K: When something **blows** you **away**,

a. they make you act in that way.

b. it impresses you greatly.

c. it is not easy to notice.

d. they have made a record of it.

e. you are aware of what is happening around you.

> **CRITICAL THINKING** **Inferences** are logical guesses about information a writer doesn't directly say. You make inferences based on information suggested—but not necessarily stated—in a text. When you make an inference, be sure there is evidence in the text to support it. For example, in paragraph E, we can infer that using animals as disaster warning systems is probably cheaper compared to other types of warning systems, even though it is not explicitly stated.

F Check (✓) the two statements that can be inferred from the excerpt below. Discuss the reasons for your answers with a partner. CRITICAL THINKING: INFERRING

"In 2014, a team of U.S. scientists studied the migration patterns of golden-winged warblers. To track the birds' movements, the researchers attached small, lightweight geolocators that recorded the birds' locations. In April, the team expected to find the warblers in the Cumberland Mountains of eastern Tennessee, where they breed and raise their young. But the birds were not there. Instead, they discovered that most of the birds had flown to Florida; one had even traveled to Cuba."

☒ 1. The scientists wanted to study the behavior of birds in Florida.

☒ 2. The researchers used geolocators to find the birds in Florida and Cuba.

☐ 3. The birds live in Tennessee the whole year round.

☐ 4. It is unusual for the birds to travel south in April.

In 2011, lemurs in the National Zoo ▷ in Washington, D.C., started making alarm calls 15 minutes before an earthquake struck the area.

DEVELOPING READING SKILLS

READING SKILL Understanding Referencing and Cohesion

Writers often use **referents** to refer to a noun or an idea that appeared previously in the passage. This helps connect ideas and avoid repetition. The noun or idea that is being referred to is called an **antecedent**.

ANTECEDENT

<u>Scientists</u> have long suspected that animals might indeed have a "sixth sense." … Until

recently, <u>they</u> have had to rely on informal reports of changes in animal behavior.

REFERENT

Referents are usually:

- pronouns (*he, she, they, it,* etc.).
- possessive adjectives (*his, her, our, its,* etc.).
- demonstrative pronouns (*this, that, these, those*).

If you are not sure what a referent is referring to, look at the earlier part of the sentence or sentences that appeared before it. When you find a noun or an idea that might be the antecedent, read the words around it. Check that the context matches the context of the sentence with the referent. The referent and the antecedent have to agree in gender and number, e.g., if the referent is *they*, look for plural nouns.

UNDERSTANDING
REFERENCING

A Read the sentences from the reading passage. Underline the antecedent that the referent in **bold** refers to.

1. In the last few days, there were no animal sightings at all. The researchers were puzzled: **this** was highly unusual behavior, especially in a rain forest area normally filled with wildlife.

2. "As far as we know, this is the first time that [we] have documented this phenomenon prior to an earthquake," says lead researcher Dr. Rachel Grant. **She** believes the findings could have important consequences for earthquake prediction.

3. Two weeks before the earthquake in Peru, a significant atmospheric change was recorded. Eight days before the quake, **it** became even more intense, …

4. In April, the team expected to find the warblers in the Cumberland Mountains of eastern Tennessee, where **they** breed and raise their young.

UNDERSTANDING
REFERENCING

B Read the paragraph from the passage. Underline the antecedent that each referent in **bold** refers to, and draw an arrow to it.

When it comes to predicting earthquakes, rodents such as rats appear to be the most sensitive animals in the rain forest. "What was interesting was that <u>rodents</u> were the first to disappear," Grant says. "**They** were nowhere to be seen eight days before the earthquake … That **they** should completely disappear was amazing." Grant believes that recent research in China and Japan may help explain why **this** happened. According to **these** studies, rats' sleeping and waking patterns are disturbed in the days leading up to an earthquake. **These** changes may alert **them** to a coming disaster.

Video

Military personnel helping residents affected by Hurricane Harvey

HURRICANES

BEFORE VIEWING

A Read the caption and look at the picture. What do you think are some effects of hurricanes? Make some notes and discuss with a partner.

PREDICTING

B Read the information below and complete the meanings of the words and phrases in **bold**.

LEARNING ABOUT THE TOPIC

Hurricanes form over warm ocean waters. When a hurricane nears the coast, it creates a **storm surge**. Wind and rain from hurricanes can cause a lot of damage, but storm surges are the most destructive aspect of this type of storm. When a hurricane **makes landfall**, a large amount of water rushes over the land and destroys structures on the shore. **Debris** then joins the fast-moving water, crashing into and damaging even more structures.

1. A storm surge is _____.

2. To make landfall is to _____.

3. Debris is _____.

C The words in **bold** below are used in the video. Read the sentences. Then match each word to its definition.

> Some hurricanes can be over 1,000 miles in **diameter**.
>
> Hurricanes can cause **catastrophic** damage, destroying buildings and killing people.
>
> Thunderstorms start to form when warm, **moist** air rises to form clouds. They are less likely to occur when the air is dry.

1. _____ (adj) a little wet

2. _____ (adj) extremely bad or destructive

3. _____ (n) the length of a straight line drawn through the center of a circle

WHILE VIEWING

UNDERSTANDING
MAIN IDEAS

A ▶ Watch the video. Check (✓) the topics that are mentioned. Three are extra.

☐ 1. what hurricanes are   ☐ 5. the effects of hurricanes

☐ 2. how hurricanes form   ☐ 6. protecting your home from a hurricane

☐ 3. where hurricanes form   ☐ 7. the biggest hurricane ever recorded

☐ 4. differences between hurricanes and cyclones   ☐ 8. how scientists try to predict hurricanes

UNDERSTANDING
DETAILS

B ▶ Watch the video again. Write short answers to the questions.

1. How is the eye of the hurricane different from the wall?

_____

2. What is a "hurricane hunter"? What does it do?

_____

3. What other kinds of technology are helping scientists to predict hurricanes?

_____

AFTER VIEWING

REACTING TO
THE VIDEO

A Have you heard about any hurricanes in the news recently? What impacts did the hurricane(s) have? Discuss with a partner.

CRITICAL THINKING:
APPLYING

B Would studying animal behavior help predict a hurricane? Which animal would you study? Discuss with a partner.

_____

_____

Reading 2

PREPARING TO READ

A The words in **blue** below are used in Reading 2. Complete the sentences with the correct form of the words. Use a dictionary to help you.

BUILDING VOCABULARY

accumulate	collapse	entire	crack	eruption
explode	threaten	pressure	continuous	vast

1. A strong hurricane can result in the destruction of a(n) ___entire___ city.

2. The smoke and ash from a volcanic ___eruption___ can spread over ___vast___ areas of land.

3. Since 1659, the Central England Temperature series has kept a(n) ___continuous___ record of temperatures in parts of England.

4. Natural disasters often ___threaten___ the lives of many people when they occur in highly populated places.

5. Earthquakes occur when ___pressure___ inside Earth's crust ___accumulate___ over time and is then released. Large earthquakes can create huge ___crack___ in roads and cause buildings to shake violently and ___collapse___.

6. In 2011, an earthquake and a tsunami caused several nuclear reactors in Japan to ___explode___, leading to a nuclear disaster.

B Discuss these questions with a partner: Have you ever seen a volcanic **eruption**? What are some volcanic eruptions you know of?

USING VOCABULARY

C The prefix *super-* means "above" or "beyond." In what two ways do you think a "supervolcano" might be different from other volcanoes? Discuss with a partner.

BRAINSTORMING

_____

_____

D Look at the photos and headings in the reading passage. What topics do you think the passage covers? Check your ideas as you read.

PREDICTING

☐ 1. what a supervolcano is

☐ 2. the effects of a supervolcano eruption

☐ 3. where the world's supervolcanoes are located

☐ 4. when Yellowstone's supervolcano might erupt

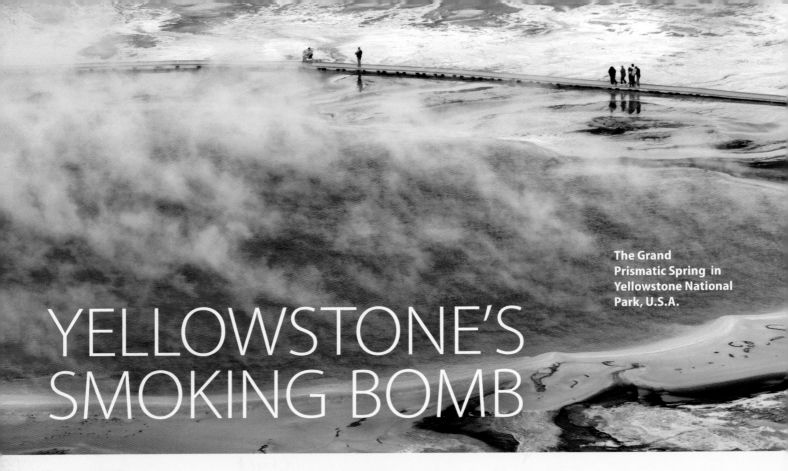

The Grand Prismatic Spring in Yellowstone National Park, U.S.A.

YELLOWSTONE'S SMOKING BOMB

🎧 1.08

Yellowstone National Park, the oldest and most famous national park in the United States, sits on top of one of the biggest volcanoes on Earth. Yellowstone's volcano is so big that many scientists call it a *supervolcano*. As the name suggests, supervolcanoes are much bigger and more powerful than ordinary volcanoes, and their eruptions can be exceptionally violent and destructive. When volcanoes erupt, they can kill plants and animals for miles around. When a supervolcano explodes, it can threaten whole species with extinction by changing the climate across the entire planet.

WHAT CAUSES A SUPERVOLCANO TO ERUPT?

No supervolcano has erupted in recorded human history. However, in the 2.1 million years that Yellowstone has sat over the supervolcano, scientists believe that the park has experienced three super-eruptions. Geologists who study Yellowstone's supervolcano have pieced together the sequence of events that probably cause a super-eruption. First, an intense plume of heat pushes up from deep within Earth. The extreme heat melts rock and creates a huge chamber a few miles below the surface. The chamber slowly fills with a pressurized mix of magma (melted rock), water vapor, carbon dioxide, and other gases. As additional magma accumulates in the chamber over thousands of years, the land on the surface above it begins to move up to form a dome, inches at a time. As the dome moves higher, cracks form along its edges. When the pressure in the magma chamber is released through the cracks in the dome, the gases suddenly explode, creating a violent super-eruption and emptying the magma chamber. Once the magma chamber is empty, the dome collapses, leaving a giant caldera, or crater, in the ground. Yellowstone's caldera, which covers a 25-by-37-mile (or 40-by-60-kilometer) area in the state of Wyoming, was formed after the last super-eruption, some 640,000 years ago.

(continued on page 90)

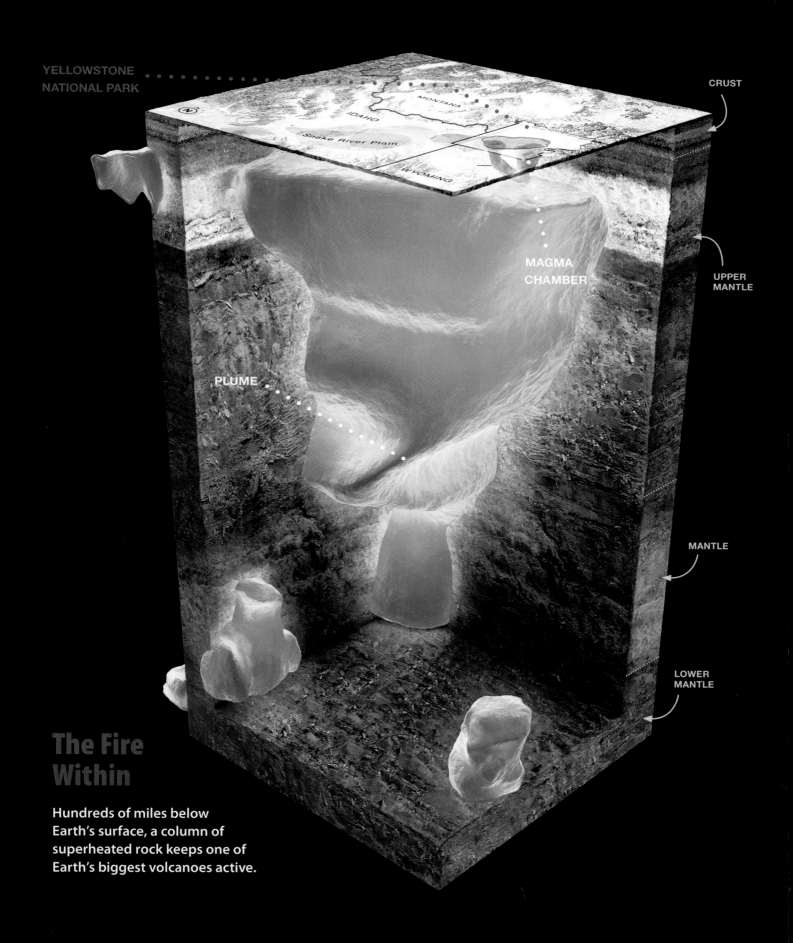

CRUST

MONTANA

IDAHO

Snake River Plain

WYOMING

MAGMA
CHAMBER

UPPER
MANTLE

PLUME

MANTLE

LOWER
MANTLE

The Fire Within

Hundreds of miles below
Earth's surface, a column of
superheated rock keeps one of
Earth's biggest volcanoes active.

A WAKING GIANT?

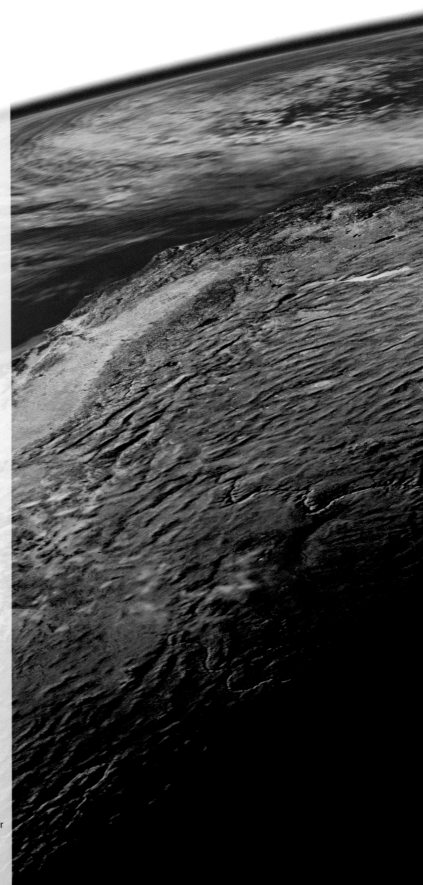

1870: Army officer Gustavus Doane explores the region that will later become Yellowstone National Park. He notices there is a huge open space— or a basin—surrounded by mountains and concludes that it is the crater of a huge extinct volcano.

1950s: Harvard graduate student Francis Boyd discovers a thick layer of heated and compacted[1] ash at Yellowstone and determines that it is the result of a geologically recent eruption.

1970s: Supervolcano expert Bob Smith of the University of Utah finds that land near the caldera has risen by some 30 inches (76 centimeters) in three decades, proving the supervolcano is alive.

1985: A number of small earthquakes strike the area, causing the land to sink. Over the next decade, it sinks eight inches (20 centimeters).

2004–2007: The ground above the caldera rises upward at rates as high as 2.8 inches (7 centimeters) a year.

2007–2010: The ground rise slows to one centimeter or less a year, but the ground has risen about 10 inches (25 centimeters) in just a few years. "It's an extraordinary uplift," says Smith, "because it covers such a large area and the rates are so high."

[1] If something is **compacted**, it is densely packed or pressed together as a result of external pressure.

Fire and debris rise from deep within Earth under Yellowstone in this artist's view of a supervolcanic eruption.

HOW VIOLENT IS A SUPER-ERUPTION?

After each super-eruption at Yellowstone, the whole planet felt the effects. Scientists theorize that gases rising high into the atmosphere mixed with water vapor to create a haze that reduced sunlight, causing a period of cooling across the globe. It is estimated that the combined debris from the three eruptions was so vast, it could have filled the Grand Canyon.

The most recent catastrophic eruption, about 640,000 years ago, poured out 240 cubic miles (1,000 cubic kilometers) of rock, lava, and ash. A column of ash rose some 100,000 feet (30 kilometers) into the atmosphere, and winds carried ash and dust across the western half of the United States and south to the Gulf of Mexico. Closer to the supervolcano, thick clouds of ash, rocks, and gas—superheated to 1,470 degrees Fahrenheit (800 degrees Celsius)—rolled over the land. This volcano's lava and debris destroyed everything within its devastating range, filling entire valleys and forming layers hundreds of feet thick.

WILL THE SUPERVOLCANO ERUPT AGAIN?

Predicting when an eruption might occur is extremely difficult, in part because scientists still do not understand all the details of what is happening under the caldera's surface. Moreover, they have kept continuous records of Yellowstone's activity only since the 1970s—a tiny slice of geologic time—making it hard to draw conclusions. However, scientists theorize that Yellowstone's magma chamber expands periodically from a plume of hot rock moving up from deep inside Earth. As the chamber expands, it pushes the land above it upward. According to this theory, when the plume of rock decreases, the magma cools and becomes solid, allowing the land above to fall back.

Scientists believe that Yellowstone has probably seen a continuous cycle of rising and falling land over the past 15,000 years. Geophysicist and supervolcano expert Bob Smith of the University of Utah believes the rise-and-fall cycle of Yellowstone's caldera will likely continue. "These calderas tend to go up and down, up and down," he says. "We call this a caldera at unrest. The net effect over many cycles is to finally get enough magma to erupt. And we don't know what those cycles are."

So is the supervolcano going to explode again? Some kind of eruption is highly likely at some point. The chances of another catastrophic super-eruption are anyone's guess. It could happen in this century, or 100,000 years from now. No one knows for sure.

THE YELLOWSTONE ERUPTIONS

Three major blasts have shaken Yellowstone National Park during the past 2 million years. The smallest of these, 1.3 million years ago, produced 280 times more material than the 1980 eruption of Mount St. Helens. After the two biggest eruptions, winds carried material from Yellowstone across much of the United States.

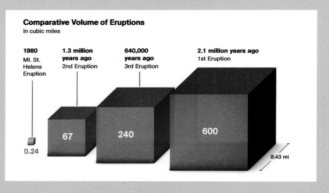

Comparative Volume of Eruptions
In cubic miles

1980 Mt. St. Helens Eruption	1.3 million years ago 2nd Eruption	640,000 years ago 3rd Eruption	2.1 million years ago 1st Eruption
0.24	67	240	600

8.43 mi

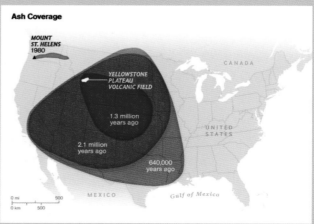

Ash Coverage

MOUNT ST. HELENS 1980

CANADA

YELLOWSTONE PLATEAU VOLCANIC FIELD

1.3 million years ago

UNITED STATES

2.1 million years ago

640,000 years ago

0 mi   500
0 km   500

MEXICO   Gulf of Mexico

UNDERSTANDING THE READING

A Complete the summary of the reading passage using suitable words. Write no more than three words in each space.

Supervolcanoes are different from normal volcanoes because they are
¹_____ in size and ²_____. One supervolcano is located
under ³_____ and has been there for at least ⁴_____.
Scientists believe that there have been three ⁵_____ during that period.
A supervolcano's eruption is so violent that the whole planet can feel its effects. The ash
and rock that it releases into the air can block ⁶_____ and cause global
temperatures ⁷_____. It is difficult to predict when a supervolcano will
erupt. Scientists think that Yellowstone's caldera has been at unrest for the past
⁸_____ years, and that there is a high chance that the supervolcano will
erupt again.

B Use information from the sidebar "The Yellowstone Eruptions" to answer the questions.

1. What is the main purpose of the information in this section?

   a. to describe the ages and sizes of several different volcanoes in North America

   b. to compare the size and extent of Yellowstone's eruptions with a more recent volcanic eruption

   c. to show how the volume of Yellowstone's eruptions has steadily increased over time

2. About how much material was produced by the most recent super-eruption?

   _____

3. Which eruption covered the largest amount of the United States with ash?

   _____

4. Which paragraphs from the reading passage does the sidebar mostly relate to?

   _____

C Check (✓) the two best inferences based on the information in paragraphs C and D. Then discuss the reasons for your answers with a partner.

☐ 1. The most recent super-eruption caused the extinction of many plant and animal species.

☐ 2. Yellowstone's supervolcano does not erupt very frequently.

☐ 3. Scientists probably found evidence of volcanic ash from the supervolcano in the western United States and the Gulf of Mexico.

UNDERSTANDING
A PROCESS

D Label the illustration below to show the stages in a supervolcano eruption (a–f).

a. The chamber becomes empty, leaving a huge crater in the ground.
b. A plume of extreme heat rises from deep within Earth.
c. Columns of ash may rise many kilometers into the air.
d. Pressure forces gases to explode upward through cracks in the dome.
e. The chamber pushes the surface of the land to form a dome.
f. The intense heat melts rock, creating a chamber just below the surface.

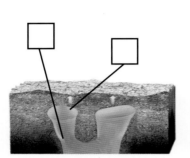
Before the Eruption

The Volcano Erupts

After the Eruption

INFERRING MEANING

E Find the following underlined words and phrases in the reading passage. Use context to identify their meanings. Then circle the best option to complete the definitions.

1. Paragraph A: You use <u>exceptionally</u> to describe something that is true to a very **large** / **slight** degree.

2. Paragraph B: To <u>piece together</u> means to **research** / **understand** how something works.

3. Paragraph E: A <u>slice</u> of something is a **section** / **demonstration** of it.

4. Paragraph E: If something happens <u>periodically</u>, it happens **once** / **several times**.

CRITICAL THINKING:
ANALYZING EVIDENCE

F Answer these questions. Then discuss with a partner.

1. What three pieces of evidence from the timeline "A Waking Giant?" show that a supervolcano exists under Yellowstone and is still alive?

_____

_____

2. Refer to paragraphs E–G. What are two reasons why it is difficult for scientists to predict when the supervolcano will erupt again?

_____

_____

Writing

EXPLORING WRITTEN ENGLISH

A Read the sentences below. For each sentence, what do the underlined words have in common in terms of their grammatical form and tense? Discuss with a partner.

NOTICING

1. Some scientists have begun <u>studying</u> and <u>recording</u> animal movements to try to prove that animals can make predictions.

2. Dr. Rachel Grant believes that prior to an earthquake, large forces <u>stress</u> Earth's surface and <u>change</u> Earth's atmosphere.

3. Yellowstone National Park is the <u>oldest</u> and <u>most famous</u> national park in the United States.

4. Supervolcanoes are <u>much bigger</u> and <u>more powerful</u> than ordinary volcanoes.

5. Before an eruption, a supervolcano's chamber slowly fills with a pressurized mix of <u>magma</u> (melted rock), <u>water vapor</u>, <u>carbon dioxide</u>, and <u>other gases</u>.

6. A volcano's <u>lava</u> and <u>debris</u> destroy everything within its devastating range.

LANGUAGE FOR WRITING Using Parallel Structures

When you join two ideas in one sentence, both ideas have to be in the same grammatical form and tense. In addition, the two parallel ideas should come immediately before and after *and*. Look at these examples.

Parallel nouns:

Idea 1: *Property gets damaged in earthquakes.*

Idea 2: *Earthquakes damage buildings.*

Property *and* ***buildings*** *get damaged in earthquakes.*

Parallel verbs:

Idea 1: *Learn about earthquake safety online.*

Idea 2: *Phone numbers for local shelters can be found online.*

You can ***learn*** *about earthquake safety and* ***find*** *phone numbers for local shelters online.*

Parallel adjectives:

Idea 1: *The people were hungry.*

Idea 2: *They also needed to sleep.*

The people were ***hungry*** *and* ***tired***.

B Complete the sentences (1–5) by combining the two ideas with parallel structures.

1. Idea 1: When it starts to rain, streets will be slippery.
   Idea 2: Slippery streets can be a danger.
   When it starts to rain, streets will be _____ and

   _____ .

2. Idea 1: People can prepare for a hurricane by buying extra food.
   Idea 2: They also need extra water.
   To prepare for a hurricane, people can _____ and

   _____ .

3. Idea 1: People need to be cautious.
   Idea 2: People aren't aware of dangers.
   People should _____ and _____
   of dangers.

4. Idea 1: People are frightened of hurricanes.
   Idea 2: Hurricanes cause damage to property.
   Hurricanes _____ people and

   _____ property.

5. Idea 1: Houses were crushed by the tornado.
   Idea 2: The tornado carried cars away.
   The tornado was so strong that it _____ and

   _____ .

WRITING SKILL Writing a Process Essay

A process essay explains how to do something, such as how to apply for financial aid or use a computer program. Each body paragraph describes one or more tasks or steps required for accomplishing the goal. The body paragraphs can be organized:

- in order of importance (in your opinion).
- chronologically (if the steps should happen in a particular time order).

Each body paragraph begins with a topic sentence that describes the task(s) or the step(s). The details in the paragraph include important information that helps the reader understand the process.

Use the following transition words and phrases to connect the body paragraphs and help the reader follow the order of the tasks or the steps.

The first step is ...   *First, ...*
Most importantly, ...   *The most important thing ...*

Second, ...   *Then, ...*   *Next, ...*
After that, ...   *Another important thing is ...*

Before doing the next step, ...   *The last step is ...*

C Put the steps below in the best order (1–6). Then write the steps out in order using appropriate transition words.

Planning for a vacation:

_____ Download movies or shows to watch on your flight.

_____ Pack your bags.

_____ Search flights and hotels.

_____ Reserve a flight and a hotel room.

_____ Choose a place to go.

_____ Check the weather.

I'm planning for a vacation. First, I need to _____

_____

_____

_____

_____

_____

D Choose one of the steps in exercise C. Brainstorm for details and examples to elaborate on it. Take some notes below.

Step: _____

Details: _____

_____

E Using your ideas in exercise D, write two to three sentences to describe the step you chose. Then share your sentences with a partner.

_____

_____

_____

_____

_____

WRITING TASK

GOAL You are going to write a process essay on the following topic:

Choose one type of natural hazard. Describe how residents of an affected city can prepare for it.

BRAINSTORMING **A** Decide on a natural hazard you will write about. List the types of risk there are for residents and the kinds of damage the natural hazard can cause. Then list ways that residents can prepare for it. Do research if necessary.

PLANNING **B** Follow these steps to make notes for your essay.

Step 1 Decide on the two most important tasks that residents should do in order to prepare for the natural disaster. State the natural hazard you are going to discuss and complete the thesis statement.

Step 2 For each body paragraph, write a topic sentence that describes one method of preparation.

Step 3 Note two or three details for each body paragraph, e.g., why this type of preparation is helpful, how it can be done, what kind of harm it might prevent.

Step 4 Make notes for a hook in the introductory paragraph. Then write a summary statement and add a final thought in the concluding paragraph.

OUTLINE

Introductory Paragraph

Hook: _____

Thesis Statement: To prepare for _____,

residents should _____ and _____.

Body Paragraphs

Topic Sentence 1: _____

_____

Details: _____

Topic Sentence 2: _____

_____

Details: _____

Concluding Paragraph

Summary Statement: _____

_____

Final Thought: _____

FIRST DRAFT **C** Use the information in your outline to write a first draft of your essay.

REVISING PRACTICE

The draft below is a process essay about ways to prepare for travel emergencies. Follow the steps to create a better second draft.

1. Add the sentences (a–c) in the most suitable spaces.
   a. In addition, travelers should pack a first-aid kit containing bandages, pain relievers, antibiotic creams, and any other necessary items.
   b. Another important thing for people to consider is what they might need in the event that they lose items such as passports and credit cards.
   c. To prepare for a travel emergency, travelers should think about their medical needs and consider what they might need in case of the theft or loss of important items.

2. Now fix the following problems (d–f) in the essay.
   d. Cross out one sentence in paragraph A that does not relate to the essay topic.
   e. Correct a mistake with a transition word or phrase in paragraph B.
   f. Correct a mistake with parallel structure in paragraph C.

A

When most people plan a vacation, they spend a lot of time choosing a hotel or deciding what sites they want to see. The best places to look for cheap flights and hotel rooms are discount travel websites. However, they may not plan for possible travel emergencies. _____

B

First importantly, thinking about medical needs beforehand can save travelers a lot of time and trouble. They should pack enough medication to last for the whole trip, so they don't have to refill prescriptions while they're traveling. They should also keep their prescription medications in the original bottles, so they will know the details of the medication if they do need to get a refill. _____

C

_____ It's a good idea to know the phone numbers of their embassies or consulates in case their passports are stolen. Travelers should also have pictures of their passports on their phones and keeping copies in different parts of their luggage. This way, it will be easier to get replacement passports if necessary. Finally, travelers should know the phone numbers of their credit card companies so they can cancel their cards immediately after they are lost or stolen.

D

If people are prepared for emergencies before they leave for a vacation, they will avoid ruining a trip with serious problems. A little bit of planning ahead of time can save travelers a lot of problems later.

D Now use the questions below to revise your essay.   REVISED DRAFT

☐ Does your introductory paragraph have a hook and a clear thesis statement?

☐ Did you include enough details in your body paragraphs to explain the tasks or steps?

☐ Did you use transition words and phrases correctly?

☐ Does your concluding paragraph have a summary statement and a final thought?

EDITING PRACTICE

Read the information below.

In sentences with parallel structure, remember that:
- the ideas have to be in the same form, so when combining sentences you may have to shift words around, change a verb tense, or change the form (e.g., change a verb to an adjective).
- the two parallel ideas should come immediately before and after *and*.

Correct one mistake with parallel structures in each of the sentences (1–5).

1. People can prepare for fires by creating an escape plan and discuss it with family members.

2. Keep important papers and putting medicine in one place.

3. If you need to take pets with you, pet carriers are important to have and extra pet food.

4. To walk around your house and identify things you will need to take.

5. Pack a bag with clothes for each family member and necessities.

FINAL DRAFT **E** **Follow these steps to write a final draft.**

1. Check your revised draft for mistakes with parallel structures.

2. Now use the checklist on page 253 to write a final draft. Make any other necessary changes.

UNIT REVIEW

Answer the following questions.

1. According to scientists, what is one reason that animals might be able to predict natural hazards?

_____

_____

_____

2. What are two ways that you can organize ideas in a process essay?

_____

_____

_____

3. Do you remember the meanings of these words? Check (✔) the ones you know. Look back at the unit and review the ones you don't know.

Reading 1:

☐ affordable   ☐ alert   ☐ deadly

☐ destruction   ☐ disaster   ☐ effectively

☐ forecast   ☐ get out   ☐ hazard

☐ throughout

Reading 2:

☐ accumulate ᴬᵂᴸ   ☐ collapse ᴬᵂᴸ   ☐ continuous

☐ crack   ☐ entire   ☐ eruption

☐ explode   ☐ pressure   ☐ threaten

☐ vast

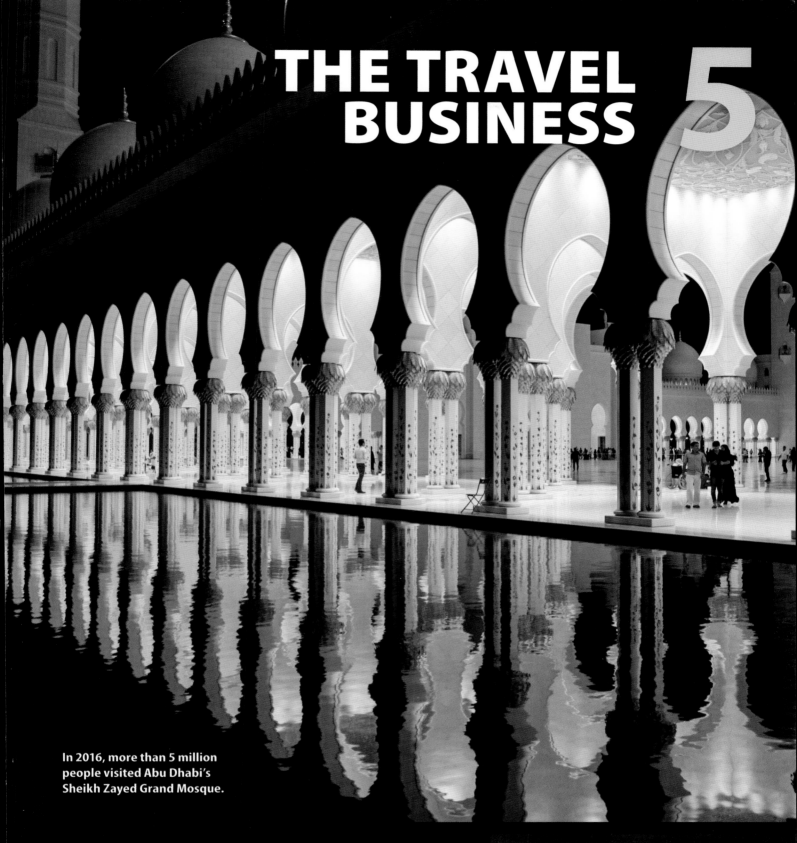

THE TRAVEL BUSINESS

5

In 2016, more than 5 million people visited Abu Dhabi's Sheikh Zayed Grand Mosque.

ACADEMIC SKILLS

READING   Analyzing causes and effects
WRITING   Writing a cause-effect essay
GRAMMAR   Using *if . . . , (then) . . .*
CRITICAL THINKING   Evaluating arguments

THINK AND DISCUSS

1   What benefits can tourism bring to a city?
2   What problems can tourism cause?

EXPLORE THE THEME

A Look at the information on these pages and answer the questions.

1. Look at the list of the top most visited cities. Why do you think so many people go to those places?
2. What are some positive effects of mass tourism?

B Match the words in yellow **to their definitions.**

_____ (v) to keep in good condition

_____ (n) the system by which a government's industry and money are organized

_____ (adj) special; very different

Osaka was the world's 17th most popular destination in 2016. Among the city's most distinctive landmarks is Shitennō-ji—one of the oldest temples in Japan.

Top 10 destination cities by international overnight visitors (2016)

1 Bangkok 21.5 million	4 Dubai 15.3 million	5 New York 12.8 million	6 Singapore 12.1 million
2 London 19.9 million	7 Kuala Lumpur 12.0 million	9 Tokyo 11.7 million	10 Seoul 10.2 million
3 Paris 18.0 million	8 Istanbul 12.0 million		

TRENDS IN TRAVEL

A recent study of global travel shows some surprising trends. While Paris and London have always been popular with businesspeople and tourists, the world's most visited city is Bangkok, which had over 21 million overnight travelers in 2016. The fastest-growing destination in terms of visitors who stay overnight is Osaka. In terms of how much money visitors spend in the city, Dubai ranks number one—visitors spent over $31 billion there in 2016.

For many of these destinations, mass tourism—large groups of people visiting popular destinations on organized trips—is critical to the success of their economy. Tourists spend money at hotels, shops, restaurants, and attractions—providing jobs for thousands of people. Tourism dollars also help cities build and maintain roads, parks, and other amenities, which benefit both visitors and locals.

Fastest-growing destination cities
(Rank in growth rate, 2016)

1	2	3
Osaka	Chengdu	Abu Dhabi

Reading 1

PREPARING TO READ

BUILDING VOCABULARY

A The words and phrases in **blue** below are used in Reading 1. Read the paragraph. Then match the correct form of each word or phrase to its definition.

Mass tourism isn't the only way to travel. One **alternative** is to experience another country by studying there. Many universities form **partnerships** with schools in other parts of the world to allow their students to learn about other cultures. Overseas students may also choose to stay in their host country during vacations, particularly if they are able to **earn a living** through part-time jobs, such as working in a café or restaurant.

1. _____ (v) to get money to pay for things that you need

2. _____ (n) a way of working with another person, group, or organization

3. _____ (n) something you can choose instead of another thing

BUILDING VOCABULARY

B Read the sentences. Choose the best definitions for the words in **blue**.

1. Many cities **preserve** their historic buildings, so tourists can see how the city used to look.
   a. to make additional copies of
   b. to protect from harm

2. It may be **necessary** to get a visa before you are allowed to enter a country.
   a. essential; required
   b. useful; recommended

3. Economic development must be **sustainable** in order to benefit future generations.
   a. able to continue in the long term
   b. able to affect many places

4. Mass tourism can have **harmful** effects on cities, such as increasing pollution levels.
   a. unusual; surprising
   b. damaging; dangerous

USING VOCABULARY

C Discuss these questions with a partner.

1. What are some **distinctive** travel destinations in your country or region?

2. Which historic places or buildings in your area have been **preserved**?

BRAINSTORMING

D What are the positive and negative effects of large numbers of tourists visiting a natural area, such as a beach or a forest? Discuss with a partner.

PREDICTING

E Read the first paragraph of the reading passage. The prefix *geo-* refers to the Earth. How do you think "geotourism" is different from mass tourism? Check your ideas as you read.

THE NEW FACE OF TOURISM

1.09

A The twenty-first century has seen significant growth in mass tourism. This growth brings an increased risk of endangering the sites that make a place unique and worth visiting. However, a new kind of tourism approach—geotourism—may offer a solution.

B Jonathan Tourtellot is founding director of the Destination Stewardship Center. Its mission is to protect and maintain the world's distinctive places through wisely managed tourism. Tourtellot is an advocate of the *geotourism* approach, a term he came up with to describe the core strategy for achieving this goal. He believes that as mass tourism continues to grow and move into places that saw few visitors in the past, geotourism will be a good long-term plan. "The challenge of managing tourism in a way that protects places instead of overrunning[1] them," says Tourtellot, "is simply going to become larger."

C Geotourism is an alternative to mass tourism, which can have harmful effects on local people and on the environment. Many of the systems that support mass tourism—large hotels, chain restaurants,[2] tour companies—are often owned and run by companies based outside the tourist areas. Chain restaurants may not always serve local food. Large tour companies do not always hire local experts and guides, even though these people might have the most insight into the area's history and culture. Much of the money made from this type of tourism does not, therefore, benefit the local economy. In addition, with mass tourism, visitors do not usually have much contact with the local people. This limits their understanding of the nature and culture of the places they visit.

D In contrast, geotourism is like a partnership between travelers and locals. For example, geotravelers stay in hotels owned by local residents who care about protecting the area and the environment. Geotravelers eat in restaurants that serve regional dishes. They buy from local merchants and craftspeople and hire local travel guides. They also try to see traditional music, dance, and theater. As a result, these travelers gain a broader understanding of the area's history and culture. Moreover, the money they spend stays in the local community. This helps local people earn a living; it is also necessary in order to protect the area for future travelers. In this way, geotourism benefits both sides of the partnership—the travelers and the locals.

[1]If a place is **overrun**, it is fully occupied.
[2]**Chain restaurants** are owned by the same company and have standardized products and services.

Geotourism Pioneer:
An Interview with Jonathan Tourtellot

Q: How would you differentiate among ecotourism, sustainable tourism, and geotourism?

Tourtellot: Ecotourism focuses specifically on natural areas. I'm convinced that there are elephants roaming Africa and trees growing in Costa Rica that would not be there without ecotourism. Sustainable tourism ... seems to say, "Keep everything the way it is." We needed a term that would bring the ecotourism principle out of its niche[3] and cover everything that makes travel interesting. Geotourism is defined as tourism that sustains or enhances the geographical character of a place—the environment, heritage, aesthetics,[4] culture, and well-being of local people.

Q: What happens when tourism is badly managed?

Tourtellot: It can destroy a place. Coasts, for example, are extremely vulnerable. Coasts are important for biodiversity because much of marine life has its nurseries[5] in coastline areas. So development there is a highly sensitive issue. Same thing goes for attractive mountainsides like the Rockies of the West. That's why when development occurs on a large scale, it's important that it be ... well planned.

Q: What happens to a destination after years of heavy traffic?

Tourtellot: Here's an example—at the Petrified Forest [in northeast Arizona], it's very easy to bend down, pick up a little bit of petrified wood, and pocket it. People think it's only one pebble[6] in such a vast area, so it makes no difference if they take it. But since millions of visitors over the years have thought the same thing, all of the pebbles have disappeared—meaning there's been an enormous loss of what makes the Petrified Forest so special. So, when you're talking about an entire location like a town, a stretch of coastline, a wild area, or a national park, it's important to listen to park rangers when they tell you where to go and not go, what to do and not do.

[3] A **niche** is a special area of demand for a product or a service.
[4] **Aesthetics** relates to the appreciation and study of beauty.
[5] Marine-life **nurseries** are places where young sea creatures can begin growing into adults.

[6] A **pebble** is a small, round stone.

According to a survey by the Destination Stewardship Center, the Norwegian Fjords are one of the world's best examples of geotourism.

Q: What happens when tourism is managed well?

Tourtellot: It can save a place. When people come [to] see something special and unique to an area—its nature, historic structures, great cultural events, beautiful landscapes, even special cuisine—they are enjoying and learning more about a destination's geographical character … [T]ravelers spend their money in a way that helps maintain the geographical diversity and distinctiveness of the place they're visiting. It can be as simple as spending your money at a little restaurant that serves a regional dish with ingredients from local farmers, rather than at an international franchise[7] that serves the same food you can get back home.

Q: How else can tourism help benefit a destination?

Tourtellot: Great tourism can build something that wasn't there before. My favorite example is the Monterey Bay Aquarium in California. It was built in a restored cannery[8] building on historic Cannery Row—which is a good example of preserving a historical building rather than destroying it. The aquarium, which has about 1.8 million visitors each year, brought people's attention to the incredible variety of sea life right off the coast of California. And it played a major role in the development of the Monterey Bay National Marine Sanctuary. Once people saw what was there, they wanted to protect it.

H

I

[7] A **franchise** is allowed to sell another company's products.

[8] A **cannery** is a factory where food is canned.

UNDERSTANDING THE READING

UNDERSTANDING KEY TERMS

A Check (✓) the three best statements to complete the definition of *geotourism*.

According to Jonathan Tourtellot, geotourism _____.

☐ 1. focuses on bringing people to natural areas

☐ 2. has positive effects on local economies

☐ 3. helps preserve the environment

☐ 4. benefits international tour companies

☐ 5. is good for both travelers and locals

UNDERSTANDING MAIN IDEAS

B Check (✓) four statements that summarize Tourtellot's main ideas.

☐ 1. Geotourism is similar to ecotourism, but is mainly concerned with controlling pollution caused by tourists.

☐ 2. Tourism that is not well planned can cause significant environmental damage, particularly along coastlines.

☐ 3. When a place has a lot of visitors over a long period of time, the visitors can destroy some of the characteristics that made the site special.

☐ 4. When tourism is well planned, people learn about the geography of an area and help support it at the same time.

☐ 5. Tourism can help preserve places that might otherwise be lost.

☐ 6. The basic idea of geotourism is "keep everything the way it is."

UNDERSTANDING PURPOSE

C Match each place mentioned in the reading passage to the main reason (a–d) Tourtellot mentions it.

_____ 1. Costa Rica

_____ 2. The Rockies

_____ 3. The Petrified Forest

_____ 4. Monterey Bay Aquarium

a. an unusual landscape that has been significantly damaged by tourism

b. a region where careful development planning is important

c. an example of how geotourism can help preserve a historical site

d. a place where ecotourism has had a positive environmental impact

---

CRITICAL THINKING Writers often make arguments by contrasting the advantages of an idea with the disadvantages. You can **evaluate** their argument by asking:

• Is there enough evidence to support each argument?

• Does the writer present both sides of the argument?

• Is the presented evidence fair and up to date?

• Does the evidence relate logically to the argument?

D Complete the notes comparing geotourism and mass tourism with suitable words.

Advantages of Geotourism	Disadvantages of Mass Tourism
• allows tourism growth to be managed in the long term	• does not promote local food or culture
• people support the _____ by using local hotels or restaurants	• people spend money that doesn't go to _____
• visitors gain a deeper understanding of the area's _____	• people gain a limited _____ of the places they visit
• careful development can help preserve _____ and educate people about the area	• unmanaged tourist numbers can cause natural areas to _____ their original beauty

E Work with a partner. Answer the questions below.

1. What might be some disadvantages of geotourism?

    _____

    _____

2. Consider the pros and cons of geotourism and mass tourism (refer to your answers in 1, exercise D, and exercise A-2 in Explore the Theme). Are you convinced by the writer's argument that geotourism is better than mass tourism? Why or why not?

    _____

    _____

The Petrified Forest receives around 800,000 visitors every year.

DEVELOPING READING SKILLS

> **READING SKILL** Analyzing Causes and Effects
>
> Recognizing causes and effects can help you understand a writer's main arguments. The following words and phrases are used to signal cause-effect relationships.
>
> **For introducing causes:**
>
> *if, because of, when, as, one effect of*
>
> **For introducing effects:**
>
> *as a result, one result (of…) is, so, therefore, consequently, (this) leads/led to*
>
> | CAUSE | EFFECT |
> |---|---|
>
> *Tourism brings money into a community.* **As a result**, *governments can make improvements that benefit local residents.*
>
> | CAUSE | EFFECT |
> |---|---|
>
> **Because of** *the money brought into a community by tourism,* *governments can make improvements that benefit local residents.*
>
> Sometimes, writers do not use signal words to show cause-effect relationships; in these cases, you need to infer the meaning from the context.

IDENTIFYING CAUSES AND EFFECTS

A Read the sentences. Underline words that signal causes and circle those that signal effects.

1. As ecotourism can bring many benefits, many local and national governments are looking at ways to preserve their distinctive natural areas.

2. In Costa Rica, for example, an interest in developing ecotourism led to the creation of several national parks and reserves where wildlife is protected.

3. The creation of national parks and reserves requires large numbers of skilled workers. Consequently, many people who are out of work may become employed.

4. The government of Costa Rica created a successful international ecotourism marketing campaign. As a result, tourism to the country increased dramatically.

ANALYZING CAUSES AND EFFECTS

B Complete the chart with the causes and effects of geotourism / mass tourism. Use information from paragraphs C and D in the passage.

Cause	Effect
1.	1. The money made does not help the local economy.
2.	2. People don't know much about the nature and culture of the places they visit.
3. Travelers eat and shop at local businesses.	3.
4. The money spent by travelers goes to the local community.	4.

ANALYZING CAUSES AND EFFECTS

C Which of the cause-effect sentence(s) in paragraphs C and D contained a signal word or phrase? Which required inferring from the context? Discuss with a partner.

Video

Giant land tortoises on
Santa Cruz island, Galápagos

GALÁPAGOS TOURISM

BEFORE VIEWING

A What effect might tourists and tourism activities have on animal species that live on remote islands? Discuss with a partner.

B Read the information about the Galápagos Islands. Then answer the questions.

The Galápagos Islands are located 620 miles (1,000 km) off the coast of Ecuador. Thousands of different species live on the islands, many of which cannot be found anywhere else on Earth. The naturalist Charles Darwin studied the animals of the Galápagos—particularly the finches (a bird species) and tortoises. From his study of finches, Darwin saw how animals change to adapt to their environments. This research inspired his development of the theory of evolution, which he described in detail in his 1859 book *On the Origin of Species*. Today, tourists from around the world are able to interact closely with the islands' animals.

1. What is special about the animals on the Galápagos Islands?

   _____

2. How did the Galápagos Islands contribute to our scientific knowledge?

   _____

C The words and phrases in **bold** below are used in the video. Read the sentences. Then match the correct form of each word or phrase to its definition.

> **Contaminants**, such as gasoline and other fuels, can contribute to water pollution.
>
> Tourism can bring **revenue** to a place, but it can also bring problems.
>
> Jonathan Tourtellot believes that by managing tourism, we can avoid **ruining** destinations for future travelers.
>
> A global cyberattack by a computer virus, WannaCry, was a **wake-up call** for many countries to strengthen their cyber security measures.

1. _____ (n) money that a company or an organization receives
2. _____ (n) a substance that makes something unsuitable for use
3. _____ (v) to destroy or severely damage something
4. _____ (n) an event that is serious enough to make people aware of a big problem

WHILE VIEWING

A ▶ Watch the video. Check (✓) the main ideas of the video.

☐ 1. Human presence on the islands has increased significantly in the last few decades.
☐ 2. Tourist revenue has been used for some major construction projects on the islands.
☐ 3. Tourism is negatively affecting the natural environment of the islands.
☐ 4. The local people have started adopting more environmentally friendly practices.

B ▶ Watch the video again. Check (✓) the actions that are being taken to make the islands greener.

☐ 1. Older oil tanks have been replaced with more modern ones.
☐ 2. The number of tourists on the islands has been restricted.
☐ 3. Gas stations have barriers to prevent oil leaks.
☐ 4. Cars will be replaced with vehicles that are more environmentally friendly.
☐ 5. The locals are reducing their waste and recycling more.

AFTER VIEWING

A Read the statements below. Which do you agree with more? Why? Discuss with a partner.

1. Banning tourists from the islands is the most effective way to protect the natural environment.

2. Tourism on the islands should be allowed, as long as more efforts are made to manage its growth.

B Work with a partner. Can you think of other ways that the environment on the Galápagos Islands could be protected? Use ideas from Reading 1 or your own ideas.

Reading 2

PREPARING TO READ

A The words in **blue** below are used in Reading 2. Read the paragraphs. Then match the correct form of each word to its definition.

BUILDING VOCABULARY

A key **objective** of geotourism is to make sure places are environmentally friendly. Some hotels, for example, not only provide **comfort** to their visitors; they also have sustainable practices such as using **renewable** energy sources like solar power for electricity. Hotel companies are also encouraged to assess the **ecological** impact of any new projects before they start building.

Another **vital** part of geotourism is to raise people's **awareness** of the history and culture of the places they visit. For example, tours may include visits to **landmarks** that have **spiritual** meaning to the local people, such as Chichén Itzá in Mexico, where ceremonies for the gods were often performed. These visits are often more **enriching** when tourists have the chance to interact with local people employed as **official** guides.

1. _____ (n) a goal

2. _____ (n) a state of ease or well-being

3. _____ (n) knowledge that something exists

4. _____ (adj) able to be replaced naturally

5. _____ (adj) necessary or extremely important

6. _____ (adj) providing more appreciation or enjoyment

7. _____ (adj) relating to a government or an organization

8. _____ (n) a building or structure with historical or cultural significance

9. _____ (adj) relating to a higher purpose rather than just material needs

10. _____ (adj) relating to the relationship between living things and their surroundings

B Think back to the last time you traveled to a new place. What was your main **objective**: to relax, to learn something, to meet people, or something else? Discuss with a partner.

USING VOCABULARY

C Skim the reading passage and answer the questions. Then check your ideas as you read.

SKIMMING

1. What types of natural places does the reading passage describe?

   _____

2. What do these places have in common? List one or two things.

   _____

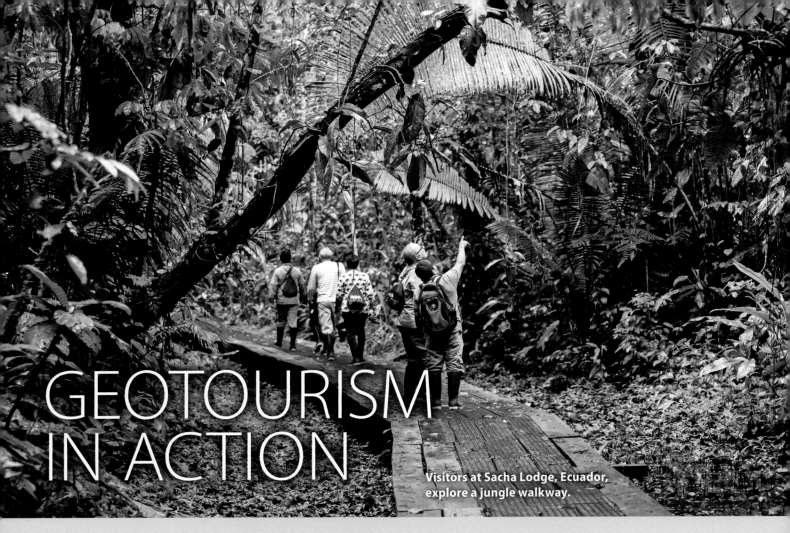

GEOTOURISM IN ACTION

Visitors at Sacha Lodge, Ecuador, explore a jungle walkway.

🎧 1.10

A As public awareness grows of the negative effects of mass tourism, more travel companies are providing options that enhance—rather than harm—local cultures and environments. The following examples from around the world show how innovative local programs can promote sustainable tourism that benefits tourists, locals, and the environment.

ECOLODGES IN ECUADOR

B Located in the Amazon basin, Ecuador is one of South America's most popular places for tourists. Ecolodges now provide a sustainable travel option for these tourists. First developed in the 1990s, an ecolodge is a type of hotel that helps local economies and protects the environment. Many of the lodges are built with renewable materials that are found locally. The lodges allow people in the community to sell locally made products to guests; some are also owned and operated by local people.

C Ecolodges not only help local economies and the environment, they also enable visitors to gain a deeper understanding of the region. There are ecolodges throughout the country, so visitors can choose to stay in the rain forest, in the mountains, or at an island beach. Visitors at Sani Lodge in the rain forest, for example, are surrounded by over 500 species of tropical birds and a thousand species of butterflies. In the Andes, guests can go hiking and explore volcanic glaciers. On the Galápagos, visitors can watch giant tortoises lay their eggs.

D These lodges let visitors interact with local people and learn about local culture, too. For example, at some ecolodges, guests learn how to make dishes using local ingredients. At Sani Lodge, local families invite guests into their homes. In 2015, the owners of Sani Lodge won the World Legacy Travel Award for their efforts to promote sustainable tourism. This kind of tourism, says company director Jascivan Carvalho, leads to "a deeper, more **enriching** experience for travelers, and for locals, whose livelihoods improve."

ADVENTURE TREKKING IN NEPAL

E Nepal has been an important trekking destination for over a hundred years. Until recently, however, most tour guides and porters were male. In 1993, three sisters—Lucky, Dicky, and Nicky Chhetri—had an idea. They were running a restaurant and lodge in Pokhara, a popular base for trekkers. When some female guests complained of poor treatment by male porters, the sisters decided to act. They would start their own trekking business—one run by women, for women. They launched their partnership—3 Sisters Adventure Trekking—with two main goals: to give local women

opportunities to work in the tourism industry, and to give female trekkers the choice of female guides for greater **comfort** and security.

F The sisters also created a nonprofit organization—Empowering Women of Nepal (EWN). The organization trains and hires local women as guides. The training program includes classes in English, health, and awareness of **ecological** issues. At the end of the program, the trainees get on-the-job experience as guides, earning the same wages as male guides. Some graduates of the program use their earnings to continue their education, while others start their own businesses.

G These improvements to the women's social and financial situations are good for both their families and the rest of the community. The interaction between local guides and tourists from all over the world creates a **vital** cultural exchange, too. "I learned to become an ambassador for my country," says one of the graduates of the program.

A local guide from 3 Sisters Adventure Trekking with a trekker on Suriya Peak in Nepal

Visitors to Uluru learn about the significance of the monument from a local guide.

CULTURAL TOURS IN AUSTRALIA

Uluru is a giant rock formation that stands in the desert of central Australia. Also known as Ayer's Rock, the famous landmark is an Australian icon and a hot spot for tourists. But for the local Anangu—meaning "we people"—Uluru is the heart of a region where they have lived for more than 20,000 years. Until recently, many visitors came to Uluru with the objective of climbing it. However, the Australian government and several tour companies are asking visitors not to do this. In fact, the government of Australia has now introduced an official policy to stop visitors from climbing the monument.

The concerns over climbing Uluru are partly because it is dangerous—the rock stands nearly 350 meters high (over 1,140 feet) and has steep sides. However, it is also a sacred site for the Anangu people, the traditional owners of the rock. For the Anangu, climbing Uluru is a spiritual experience. The government's and tour companies' efforts have had a positive effect. While 74 percent of visitors climbed Uluru in 1990, that number dropped to less than 30 percent by 2015.

Adventure Tours and SEIT Outback Australia are just two of the companies that work to educate visitors about the culture of Uluru. Some of these tour companies hire indigenous guides who can share the perspectives of the local people. Instead of taking tourists to the top of the rock, tour guides lead tourists around Uluru on the paths that Anangu ancestors walked. The guides tell traditional stories about how the world was born and how people are connected to the land. Through these travel experiences, visitors can leave Uluru culturally richer than when they arrived.

UNDERSTANDING THE READING

A Look at the main ideas (1–6) from the reading passage. Match each section of the passage (a–c) with two main ideas.

UNDERSTANDING MAIN IDEAS

a. Ecolodges in Ecuador

b. Adventure Trekking in Nepal

c. Cultural Tours in Australia

_____ 1. The main focus is on providing employment for local women and services for female travelers.

_____ 2. Visitors stay in a type of hotel accommodation that benefits the environment and the financial well-being of local communities.

_____ 3. An education program helps local people learn skills that they can use in their communities.

_____ 4. Visitors have the opportunity to experience a wide variety of natural environments.

_____ 5. Greater awareness of local concerns has reduced the negative impact of tourism on the site.

_____ 6. Tour guides emphasize how the site is culturally and historically significant for the local people.

B Match each paragraph or section from the passage to the best description (1–7).

UNDERSTANDING DETAILS

| B | C | D | E | F–G | H–I | J |

_____ 1. welcoming visitors into local homes

_____ 2. the evolution of a new type of green travel lodge

_____ 3. a wide variety of environmental experiences on offer

_____ 4. a training program that offers local women a better future

_____ 5. understanding a place from a traditional cultural perspective

_____ 6. the origins of a more gender-balanced approach to trekking

_____ 7. reasons why climbing a sacred landmark is now discouraged

Uluru is one of Australia's most well-known landmarks.

C Find and underline the following words and phrases in **bold** in the reading passage. Use context to identify their meanings. Then write the part of speech and your own definition of each word or phrase.

1. **livelihood** (paragraph D) Part of speech: _____

   Meaning: _____

   _____

2. **ambassador** (paragraph G) Part of speech: _____

   Meaning: _____

   _____

3. **hot spot** (paragraph H) Part of speech: _____

   Meaning: _____

   _____

4. **indigenous** (paragraph J) Part of speech: _____

   Meaning: _____

   _____

ANALYZING CAUSES AND EFFECTS

D Underline the word(s) that signal a cause-effect relationship in the excerpt below. What effect does ecotourism have on travelers and locals? Discuss with a partner.

Director of the company, Jascivan Carvalho, says that this kind of travel experience can lead to

"a deeper, more enriching experience for travelers, and for locals, whose livelihoods improve."

CRITICAL THINKING: SYNTHESIZING

E Read Jonathan Tourtellot's definition of geotourism from Reading 1. What are some examples from the reading that relate to his definition? Note them in the chart.

"Geotourism is defined as tourism that sustains or enhances the geographical character of a place—the environment, heritage, aesthetics, culture, and well-being of local people."

Ecolodges in Ecuador	Adventure Trekking in Nepal	Cultural Tours in Australia

CRITICAL THINKING: EVALUATING/ JUSTIFYING

F Which of the three destinations do you think is the best example of geotourism? Why? Note your ideas and discuss your reasons in a small group.

Place: _____

Reason(s): _____

_____

Writing

EXPLORING WRITTEN ENGLISH

A Read the sentences and underline the part that describes a cause. Circle the part that describes an effect.

NOTICING

1. If tourists stay at large international hotels, they often interact less with locals.

2. Tourists don't necessarily help the local economy if they only eat at chain restaurants.

LANGUAGE FOR WRITING Using *if…, (then)…*

One way to express a cause-effect relationship that is generally true is to use sentences with *if*. In these sentences, the *if*-clause introduces a condition or cause that leads to the effect or result expressed in the other clause.

> CAUSE | EFFECT
> ***If*** *tourism is managed well*, *both tourists and local people benefit.*

You can reverse the order of the clauses.

> EFFECT | CAUSE
> *Both tourists and local people benefit* ***if*** *tourism is managed well*.

You can also use a modal (*can, should, might, must*) in the effect clause.

> CAUSE | EFFECT
> ***If*** *tourism is badly managed*, *it* ***can*** *destroy a place.*

Note: Use a comma when the *if*-clause comes first. Use the present tense in the *if*-clause and the present tense or a modal in the effect clause.

B Underline the sentence in each pair (1–4) that is a cause. Then combine the sentences using *if*-clauses.

1. You buy locally made products. You support the local economy.

   _____

2. Forests and beaches might be ruined. Too many people visit them.

   _____

3. Female trekkers feel more comfortable and safe. The porters are female.

   _____

4. Tourists can learn about local customs. They stay at an ecolodge.

   _____

C Use your own ideas to complete each sentence with a cause or an effect.

1. If _____, it may harm the environment.

2. If tourists use local guides, _____.

3. Visitors can have an enriching travel experience if _____.

4. _____ if you meet locals when you travel.

WRITING SKILL Writing a Cause-Effect Essay

One type of cause-effect essay explains how a situation (a cause) produces another situation (an effect). For example, an essay could explain the effects of population growth on an area. The thesis statement in this type of essay states that the focus is on the effects of a particular cause.

In a cause-effect essay that focuses on effects, each body paragraph includes a topic sentence that states the effect. One body paragraph could focus on the most important effect; the next paragraph could focus on a less important effect. Another way to organize body paragraphs is to focus first on the effects on one group (e.g., humans), and then focus on a different group (e.g., animals) in another paragraph.

A well-developed body paragraph includes at least two supporting ideas that include reasons, facts, and examples to help a reader understand your topic sentence. One strategy for adding effective details is to think about questions (*who, why, when, where, what*) that a reader might have about your topic sentence. If your supporting ideas do not adequately answer these questions, then you should add more details.

ANALYZING A
CAUSE-EFFECT
OUTLINE

D The paragraph outline below is for an essay about how vacation rentals (houses that are rented to tourists) affect cities. Use the notes (1–4) to complete the outline.

1. neighborhood businesses lose money

2. may have to lay off employees or shorten their hours

3. they can harm neighborhoods

4. more vulnerable to burglars

Topic Sentence: *One negative effect of vacation rentals is that _____.*

Supporting Idea 1: *changes the character of a neighborhood*

Details:

• *neighborhoods become empty on weekdays / during off-peak*

• _____

Supporting Idea 2: _____

Details:

• *local businesses don't have enough customers in off-season*

• _____

E The draft paragraph below is about the effects of the redevelopment of a national park. A reader has noted some questions asking for more information. Add the details (a–d) that the writer could use to improve the paragraph.

One positive effect of the redevelopment of Ghana's Kakum National Park was that it greatly improved the local economy. ▭ In the 1990s, Conservation International formed partnerships to make the park more attractive to tourists. ▭ These improvements had positive financial effects on the community. ▭ When the project was finished, there were many more visitors to the park. ▭ This increase in tourism continues to bring money into the local economy.

Why did the park need to be redeveloped?

How was the park made attractive to tourists?

How did the community benefit?

How many more visitors were there?

a. fewer than 1,000 visitors in 1991; over 180,000 a year today
b. local people did the work; the project used local materials
c. had suffered for many years from deforestation and lack of investment
d. built visitors' center, wildlife exhibitions, restaurants, shops, camping facilities, a canopy walk—a special walkway (takes visitors through treetops of rain forest)

F Rewrite the paragraph, inserting the information from the notes in the highlighted spaces.

WRITING TASK

GOAL You are going to write a cause-effect essay on the following topic:
What are the positive—or negative—effects of tourism on a place that you know well?

BRAINSTORMING **A** Think of a place you know well that is popular with tourists. List some positive and negative effects that tourists have on this place.

PLANNING **B** Follow these steps to make notes for your essay.

Step 1 Decide whether to write about the positive or the negative effects in your essay. Write your thesis statement in the outline.

Step 2 Choose two effects and note them in the outline.

Step 3 Add two supporting ideas and details about each effect.

Step 4 Write a summary statement and add a final thought.

OUTLINE

Introductory Paragraph

Thesis Statement: _____

_____

Body Paragraphs

Effect 1: _____

Supporting Idea 1 / Details: _____

_____

Supporting Idea 2 / Details: _____

_____

Effect 2: _____

Supporting Idea 1 / Details: _____

_____

Supporting Idea 2 / Details: _____

_____

Concluding Paragraph

Summary Statement: _____

_____

Final Thought: _____

FIRST DRAFT **C** Use the information in the outline to write a first draft of your essay.

REVISING PRACTICE

The draft below is a cause-effect essay about the effects of vacation rentals on cities. Follow the steps to create a better second draft.

1. Add the sentences (a–c) in the most suitable spaces.
   a. In some cities, the vacation rental business has reduced the number of available apartments by 20 to 30 percent.
   b. Vacation rentals also have negative effects on housing in a community.
   c. As a result, they may have to lay off some of their employees or limit their hours.

2. Now fix the following problems (d–f) in the essay.
   d. Correct a mistake with an *if …* , *(then) …* sentence in paragraph B.
   e. Cross out one sentence in paragraph C that does not relate to the essay topic.
   f. Correct a mistake with an *if …* , *(then) …* sentence in paragraph C.

A

In the sharing economy, anyone can be an entrepreneur. People can make money with ridesharing, by renting out their cars, or even by renting out their homes. While allowing people to stay in your home for a few days a month might be a nice way to make some extra money, vacation rentals have negative effects on communities.

B

One negative effect of vacation rentals is that they can harm neighborhoods. For example, they can change the character of neighborhoods, particularly those in popular destinations. Low numbers of tourists on weekdays or in the off-peak season can mean nearly empty neighborhoods, making the areas easy targets for burglars. Vacation rentals can also cause neighborhood businesses to lose money. If vacation rentals are empty for days at a time, so small grocers and other neighborhood businesses don't have a lot of customers. _____

C

_____ First of all, short-term vacation rentals can cause housing shortages, as landlords rent apartments out to tourists instead of making them available to permanent residents. _____ In addition, vacation rentals drive up housing prices in a community. If there are fewer apartments available rents tend to go up, forcing people with average incomes to move outside of the city. Rental companies don't always know everything about the home or apartment owners' backgrounds.

D

Short-term vacation rentals have harmful effects on communities. They can negatively impact the character and economy of a neighborhood, and lead to housing shortages and higher rents. When tourism takes over a neighborhood and drives local residents away, is it even the same place anymore?

D **Now use the questions below to revise your essay.**

☐ Does your introduction have a clear thesis statement?
☐ Did you include enough details to explain the effects in your body paragraphs?
☐ Do all your sentences relate to the thesis statement?
☐ Does your concluding paragraph have a summary statement and a final thought?

EDITING PRACTICE

Read the information below.

In sentences with *if*-clauses that describe general truths, remember:
• that the *if*-clause introduces the condition or cause.
• to use a comma after the *if*-clause when it comes first in a sentence.
• to use the present tense in the *if*-clause, and the present tense or a modal in the effect clause.

Correct one mistake with *if*-clauses in each of the sentences (1–5).

1. If prices are too high people might stop traveling.

2. If travel journalists will write about the importance of protecting destinations, they might educate tourists.

3. If tourists only eat at chain restaurants, they didn't learn anything about local food.

4. Tourists show disrespect to the local culture, if they climb Uluru.

5. Local communities can benefit if tourism will promote local businesses.

FINAL DRAFT **E** **Follow these steps to write a final draft.**

1. Check your revised draft for mistakes with *if*-clauses.
2. Now use the checklist on page 253 to write a final draft. Make any other necessary changes.

UNIT REVIEW
Answer the following questions.

1. What are two things you learned about geotourism?

_____

_____

_____

2. What are some signal words or phrases that introduce causes or effects?

_____

_____

_____

3. Do you remember the meanings of these words? Check (✔) the ones you know. Look back at the unit and review the ones you don't know.

Reading 1:

☐ alternative **AWL**   ☐ distinctive **AWL**   ☐ earn a living
☐ economy **AWL**   ☐ harmful   ☐ maintain **AWL**
☐ necessary   ☐ partnership **AWL**   ☐ preserve
☐ sustainable **AWL**

Reading 2:

☐ awareness **AWL**   ☐ comfort   ☐ ecological
☐ enriching   ☐ landmark   ☐ objective **AWL**
☐ official   ☐ renewable   ☐ spiritual
☐ vital

VOCABULARY EXTENSION   UNIT 1

WORD LINK *pre-*

Words that begin with the prefix *pre-* mean "before in time." For example, *previously* means "before the time period that you are talking about." *Pre-* can be added to some common root words. For example, *preview* means "to see a part of something before watching the whole thing."

Complete each sentence with the words below. One word is extra.

predict	prepare	preschool	prevent	preview	previous

1. It is a good idea to _____ some slides before giving a presentation.

2. Scientists are developing apps that can _____ a person's behavior better than a human can. For example, the app can tell if a customer will buy a product again.

3. For many entry-level jobs, no _____ experience is required.

4. To _____ conflict in a workplace, try to avoid aggressive behavior with your co-workers.

5. Movie companies often upload a short video online to give people a _____ of an upcoming movie and get them excited about it.

VOCABULARY EXTENSION   UNIT 2

WORD LINK *-ist*

Some nouns that end in *-ist* can refer to someone who works in a specific academic or professional field. An *archaeologist*, for example, works in the field of archaeology. In general, for words ending in a vowel or *-y*, drop the vowel or *-y* and add *-ist*.

Complete each sentence with the correct noun form of the underlined word.

1. Someone who writes <u>novels</u> is a _____ .

2. Someone who produces <u>art</u> is an _____ .

3. Someone who looks at how the <u>economy</u> works is an _____ .

4. Someone who provides <u>therapy</u> to other people is a _____ .

5. Someone who plays the <u>piano</u> as a job is a _____ .

VOCABULARY EXTENSION   UNIT 3

WORD PARTNERS Expressions with *income*

Below are some common expressions with the word *income*.

annual income: the amount of money you earn in a year

source of income: where you get your money from, e.g., a salary, investments, etc.

income tax: a percentage the government takes from your income in the form of taxes

disposable income: the amount of money you have left after paying taxes

income inequality: a situation where there is a difference in income levels between the highest and lowest earners

Complete each sentence with the expressions from the box above.

1. Rent from people living in property you own can be an additional _____.

2. In the United States, the gap between top earners and low-wage earners is very large. This _____ concerns some economists.

3. If your _____ is $100,000 a year and you have to pay _____ of 20 percent, your _____ is $80,000.

VOCABULARY EXTENSION   UNIT 4

WORD FORMS Changing Nouns/Adjectives into Verbs with *-en*

Some nouns and adjectives can be made into verbs by adding *-en*. The suffix *-en* means "to cause to be or have." For example, *threaten* means "to cause threats."

Circle the correct form of the word to complete each sentence.

1. Hurricanes **threat** / **threaten** many parts of the world.

2. Hurricanes gain **strength** / **strengthen** over warm waters.

3. After hurricanes make landfall, they usually **weak** / **weaken**.

4. Hurricanes often produce a storm surge—extremely high waves of seawater that cause coastal flooding. The storm surge produced by Hurricane Sandy had a **height** / **heighten** of over four meters.

5. A hurricane brings extreme clouds and heavy rainfall. After the storm passes, the sky **lights** / **lightens** and residents can start cleaning up.

VOCABULARY EXTENSION   UNIT 5

WORD FORMS Adjectives and Nouns Ending In -*ive*

Most words ending in -*ive* are adjectives, though some can also be used as nouns. For instance, *alternative* can be used as an adjective (*There is an alternative plan.*) or a noun (*The alternative won't work.*).

Read the sentences below. Label each underlined word as N if it is a noun or A if it is an adjective.

1. The <u>distinctive</u> design of the Eiffel Tower makes it a well-known icon worldwide.

2. One of the <u>objectives</u> of sustainable tourism is to manage tourist destinations in a way that preserves their original state.

3. The Mayan are <u>native</u> people who live in modern-day Mexico, Honduras, and Guatemala.

4. Many companies hire sales <u>representatives</u> to sell their products to customers.

5. Companies with a strong online presence have a <u>relative</u> advantage over those companies that do not.

6. Solar power is one example of an <u>alternative</u> energy source.

Independent Student Handbook

TIPS FOR READING FLUENTLY

Reading slowly, one word at a time, makes it difficult to get an overall sense of the meaning of a text. As a result, reading becomes more challenging and less interesting. In general, it is a good idea to first skim a text for the gist, and then read it again more closely so that you can focus on the most relevant details. Use these strategies to improve your reading speed:

- Read groups of words rather than individual words.

- Keep your eyes moving forward. Read through to the end of each sentence or paragraph instead of going back to reread words or phrases.

- Skip functional words (articles, prepositions, etc.) and focus on words and phrases carrying meaning—the content words.

- Use clues in the text—such as **bold** words and words in *italics*—to help you know which parts might be important and worth focusing on.

- Use section headings, as well as the first and last lines of paragraphs, to help you understand how the text is organized.

- Use context clues, affixes, and parts of speech—instead of a dictionary—to guess the meaning of unfamiliar words and phrases.

TIPS FOR READING CRITICALLY

As you read, ask yourself questions about what the writer is saying, and how and why the writer is presenting the information at hand.

Important critical thinking skills for academic reading and writing:

- **Analyzing:** Examining a text in close detail in order to identify key points, similarities, and differences.
- **Applying:** Deciding how ideas or information might be relevant in a different context, e.g., applying possible solutions to problems.
- **Evaluating:** Using evidence to decide how relevant, important, or useful something is. This often involves looking at reasons for and against something.
- **Inferring:** "Reading between the lines"; in other words, identifying what a writer is saying indirectly, or *implicitly*, rather than directly, or *explicitly*.
- **Synthesizing:** Gathering appropriate information and ideas from more than one source and making a judgment, summary, or conclusion based on the evidence.
- **Reflecting:** Relating ideas and information in a text to your own personal experience and viewpoints.

TIPS FOR NOTE-TAKING

Taking notes will help you better understand the overall meaning and organization of a text. Note-taking also enables you to record the most important information for future uses— such as when you are preparing for an exam or completing a writing assignment. Use these techniques to make your note-taking more effective:

- As you read, underline or highlight important information such as dates, names, and places.
- Take notes in the margin. Note the main idea and supporting details next to each paragraph. Also note your own ideas or questions about the paragraph.
- On a separate piece of paper, write notes about the key points of the text in your own words. Include short headings, key words, page numbers, and quotations.
- Use a graphic organizer to summarize a text, particularly if it follows a pattern such as cause-effect, comparison-contrast, or chronological sequence. See page 108 for an example.
- Keep your notes brief by using these abbreviations and symbols. Don't write full sentences.

approx.	approximately	→	leads to / causes
e.g./ex.	example	↑	increases / increased
i.e.	that is / in other words	↓	decreases / decreased
etc.	and others / and the rest	*& or +*	and
Ch.	Chapter	*b/c*	because
p. (pp.)	page (pages)	*w/*	with
re:	regarding, concerning	*w/o*	without
incl.	including	=	is the same as
excl.	excluding	>	is more than
info	information	<	is less than
yrs.	years	~	is approximately / about
para.	paragraph	∴	therefore

TIPS FOR LEARNING VOCABULARY

You often need to use a word or phrase several times before it enters your long-term memory. Here are some strategies for successfully learning vocabulary:

- Use flash cards to test your knowledge of new vocabulary. Write the word you want to learn on one side of an index card. Write the definition and/or an example sentence that uses the word on the other side.

- Use a vocabulary notebook to note down a new word or phrase. Write a short definition of the word in English and the sentence where you found it. Write another sentence of your own that uses the word. Include any common collocations (see *Word Partners* in the Vocabulary Extensions).

- Make word webs or word maps.

- Use memory aids, or mnemonics, to remember a word or phrase. For example, if you want to learn the idiom *keep an eye on someone*, which means "to watch someone carefully," you might picture yourself putting your eyeball on someone's shoulder so that you can watch the person carefully. The stranger the picture is, the more likely you will remember it!

Prefix	Meaning	Example
com- / con-	with	compile
con-	together, with	constitute
em- / en-	making, putting	empower, endanger
ex-	away, from, out	explode
in-	not	independent
inter-	between	interact
pre-	before	preview
re-	back, again	restore
trans-	across	transfer
un-	not	unclear
vid- / vis-	seeing	video, vision

Suffix	Part of Speech	Example
-able	adjective	affordable
-al	adjective	traditional
-ate	verb	generate
-ed	adjective	involved
-ent / -ant	adjective	confident, significant
-er	noun	researcher
-ful	adjective	harmful
-ive	adjective	inventive
-ize	verb	criticize
-ly	adverb	definitely
-ment	noun	replacement
-tion	noun	determination

TIPS FOR ACADEMIC WRITING

There are many types of academic writing (descriptive, argumentative/persuasive, narrative, etc.), but most types share similar characteristics. Generally, in academic writing, you should:

- write in full sentences.
- use formal English. (Avoid slang or conversational expressions such as *kind of*.)
- be clear and coherent—keep to your main point; avoid technical words that the reader may not know.
- use signal words or phrases and conjunctions to connect your ideas. (See examples below.)
- have a clear point (main idea) for each paragraph.
- use a neutral point of view—avoid overuse of personal pronouns (*I*, *we*, *you*) and subjective language such as *nice* or *terrible*.
- use facts, examples, and expert opinions to support your argument.
- avoid using abbreviations or language used in texting. (Use *that is* rather than *i.e.*, and *in my opinion*, not *IMO*.)
- avoid using contractions. (Use *is not* rather than *isn't*.)
- avoid starting sentences with *or*, *and*, or *but*.

Signal Words and Phrases

Use signal words and phrases to connect ideas and to make your writing more academic.

Giving personal opinions	Giving details and examples	Linking ideas
In my opinion, …	An example of this is …	Furthermore, …
I (generally) agree that …	Specifically, …	Moreover, …
I think/feel (that) …	For instance, …	In addition, …
I believe (that) …		Additionally, …
		For one thing, …

Presenting similar ideas	Presenting contrasting views	Giving reasons
Similarly, …	On the other hand, …	This is because (of) …
Both … and …	In contrast, …	This is due to …
Like … , …	While it may be true that …	One reason (for this) is …
Likewise, …	Despite the fact that …	
	Even though …	

Describing causes and effects	Describing a process	Concluding
Therefore, …	First (of all), …	In conclusion, …
As a result, …	Then / Next / After that, …	In summary, …
Because of this, …	As soon as …	To conclude, …
If … , then …	Once …	To summarize, …
	Finally, …	

Writing Citations

Below are some examples of how to cite **print sources** according to the American Psychological Association Style (see also *Language for Writing* in Unit 8 for information on citing websites).

Guidelines	Reference entry	In-text citation
For an **article**, include: the author's name, year and month of publication, article title, the name of the magazine/journal, and page references.	White, M. (2011, June). Brimming pools. *National Geographic*, 100–115.	(White, 2011) White (2011) says …
For a **book**, include: the author's name, year of publication, title of the book, the location of the publisher (if known), and the name of the publisher.	Hawking, S. (1988). *A brief history of time*. New York, NY: Bantam.	(Hawking, 1988) Hawking (1988) says …
If there are **two authors**, use & to list their names.	Sherman, D., & Salisbury, J. (2008). *The west in the world: Renaissance to present*. New York, NY: McGraw-Hill.	(Sherman & Salisbury, 2008) Sherman and Salisbury (2008) say …
For a **book that is not the first edition**, include the edition number after the title.	Turnbull, C. M. (2009). *A history of modern Singapore, 1819–2005*, (3rd ed.). Singapore: NUS Press.	(Turnbull, 2009) According to Turnbull (2009), …

TIPS FOR EDITING

Capitalization and Punctuation

- Capitalize the content words in titles. Don't capitalize articles such as *the* or prepositions such as *in* and *on*, unless they are the first word of a title (e.g., *The Power of Creativity*).
- Avoid using exclamation marks (!) to indicate strong feelings such as surprise or joy. They are generally not used in academic writing.
- Use quotation marks (" ") to indicate the exact words used by someone else. (*"Our pleasures are really ancient," says psychologist Nancy Etcoff.*)

Other Proofreading Tips

- Print out your draft and read it out loud. Use a colored pen to make corrections so you can see them easily when you write your next draft.
- Have someone else read your draft and give you comments or ask you questions.
- When using a computer's spell-check function, make sure you agree with the correction before you accept the change.
- Keep a list of spelling and grammar mistakes that you commonly make so that you can be aware of them as you edit your draft.
- Check for frequently confused words:

  - *there, their*, and *they're*
  - *its* and *it's*
  - *your* and *you're*
  - *then* and *than*

  - *whose* and *who's*
  - *where, wear, we're*, and *were*
  - *affect* and *effect*

  - *quit, quiet*, and *quite*
  - *write* and *right*
  - *through, though*, and *thorough*

EDITING CHECKLIST

Use the checklist to find errors in the second draft of your writing task for each unit.

	Unit				
	1	2	3	4	5
1. Did you use capitalization correctly, e.g., for the first word of a sentence, for proper nouns, etc.?					
2. Do your subjects and verbs agree?					
3. Are commas used in the right places?					
4. Do all possessive nouns have an apostrophe?					
5. Is the spelling of places, people, and other proper nouns correct?					
6. Did you check for frequently confused words? (see examples in the *Tips for Editing* section)					
7. Did you use appropriate signal words and phrases to introduce and connect ideas? (see examples in the *Tips for Academic Writing* section)					
8. For essays that require research and the use of information from external sources, did you cite all sources properly? (see examples in the *Writing Citations* section)					

GRAMMAR REFERENCE

UNIT 3
Language for Writing: Using the Simple Past and the Present Perfect

Simple Past

- describes completed actions or events in the past
- often used with time expressions, e.g., *yesterday*, *last week*

> The scientists **gave** a presentation about the research paper **last year**.
> (The presentation was completed at a specific time in the past.)

Present Perfect

1. describes past actions or events where the specific time is unimportant or unknown

> The scientists **have made** some interesting discoveries.
> (The discoveries are more important than when they were made).

2. describes actions or events that happened in the past and that may continue into the future

> The scientists **have given** several presentations about the project this year.
> (The scientists may give more presentations before the end of the year).

3. can be used with time expressions such as *for*, *since*, and *in the* + [time period] to describe actions or events that started in the past and continue to the present

> The project **has generated** a lot of media interest **in the past month**.

Past Participle Forms of Commonly Used Irregular Verbs		
become—become	fall—fallen	read—read
begin—begun	find—found	say—said
bring—brought	get—gotten	see—seen
build—built	give—given	speak—spoken
buy—bought	have—had	take—taken
choose—chosen	hear—heard	tell—told
do—done	know—known	think—thought
eat—eaten	make—made	write—written

VOCABULARY INDEX

Word	Unit	CEFR Level	Word	Unit	CEFR Level	Word	Unit	CEFR Level
accumulate*	4	C2	crucial*	7	B2	gear (n)	10	B2
acquire*	9	B2	currently	7	B2	gender*	1	B2
affordable	4	C1	cut down on	7	B2	general	8	B1
aggressive	1	B2				generally	1	B1
alert (v)	4	C1	deadly	4	B2	generate*	7	B2
alter* (v)	10	B2	decline* (n)	8	B2	gesture (n)	6	C1
alternative* (n)	5	B2	deliberately	6	B2	get out	4	B1
ambitious	1	B2	demonstrate*	10	B2	growth	3	B2
analysis*	2	B2	dense	3	B2			
anticipate*	9	C1	descend	10	B2	harmful	5	B2
archaeologist	2	C1	destruction	4	B2	have to do with	6	B2
artificial	8	B2	detective	2	B1	hazard (n)	4	C1
aspect*	3	B2	determination	10	B2	heal	2	B2
assume*	10	B2	determine	2	C1	highly	9	B2
attempt (n)	3	B1	die out	9	B2			
awareness*	5	C1	disaster	4	B2	identity*	2	B2
			discipline (v)	1	B2	income*	3	B2
basically	3	B2	distinctive*	5	C1	increasingly	3	B2
behavior	1	B1	downside	6	C1	industrial	3	B2
breakthrough	8	B2				instantly	10	B2
			earn a living	5	B2	intense*	1	C1
care for	1	B2	ecological	5	B2	interact	1	B2
carry out	2	B1	economy*	5	B2	interpret*	6	B2
civilization	8	B2	effectively	4	B2	inventive	8	-
collapse* (v)	4	B2	emit	7	C2	invest*	7	B2
combination	2	B2	emphasize*	6	B2			
combine	9	B2	enhance*	3	C1	landmark	5	C1
comfort (n)	5	B2	enriching	5	C1	lead to	9	B2
commit*	2	B2	entire	4	B2	limited	7	B1
competence	9	C1	eruption	4	C2	linguistic	9	C1
compile*	8	C1	establish	1	B2			
concentration*	3	B2	examine	2	B2	maintain*	5	B2
concept*	8	B2	exceptional	7	B2	major* (adj)	7	B2
conflict (n)	1	B2	exhaust (v)	7	C1	majority*	3	B2
consciously	10	B2	existing	8	B1	manage to	8	B1
considerably*	9	B2	expand*	9	B2	manual* (n)	8	B2
constitute*	9	C1	expedition	10	B1	mention (v)	2	B1
consume*	7	B2	experimental	8	C2	method*	8	B1
consumption*	3	C1	explode	4	B1	misleading	6	B2
context*	6	B2	express (v)	9	B2	moreover	2	B2
continuous	4	B2	extended family	1	B2	motivation*	1	B2
convert* (v)	7	B2				mystery	2	B1
convey	6	C1	fate	10	B2			
crack (n)	4	B2	faulty	6	B2	native (adj)	9	B2
crisis	10	B2	focus on*	7	B2	necessary	5	B1
critically	9	B2	forecast (v)	4	B1	neutral*	6	C1
criticize	1	B2	furthermore*	9	B2	nevertheless*	6	B2

Target vocabulary items in this split edition are in blue.

Word	Unit	CEFR Level	Word	Unit	CEFR Level	Word	Unit	CEFR Level
objective* (adj)	6	B2	replace	1	B1	tend to	3	B2
objective* (n)	5	B2	replacement	8	B2	terrifying	10	B2
observe	1	B2	reveal*	2	B2	threaten	4	B2
obtain*	2	B2	roughly	9	B2	throughout	4	B2
official (adj)	5	B2	safety	3	B2	treat (v)	1	B2
partnership*	5	B2	sample (n)	2	B2	unclear	2	B2
perspective*	9	C1	seek	8	B2	universal	6	B2
phenomenon*	3	C1	sensation	10	B2	urban	3	B2
pioneer (n)	8	C2	separate (v)	10	B1	vanish	7	B2
political	9	B1	shrink (v)	7	B2	varied*	3	B2
practical	7	B2	slope (n)	10	B2	vast	4	B2
preserve	5	B2	social structure	1	B2	version*	10	B2
pressure (n)	4	B2	spiritual (adj)	5	B2	vision	6	B2
previously	1	B1	spread (v)	8	B2	vital	5	B2
productive	3	B2	spread out (v)	3	B2	worldwide	7	B2
propose	6	B2	stand out	6	B2			
prove	2	B1	statistic*	6	C1			
publication*	6	B2	status	1	C1			
rapidly	9	B2	suburb	3	B2			
rate (n)	9	B2	suffer from	2	B1			
recall (v)	10	B2	summit (n)	10	C1			
reduction	7	B2	survival	8	B2			
regulate*	7	C1	suspect (n)	2	B2			
reject* (v)	8	B2	sustainable*	5	C1			
related to	7	C1	take over	10	B2			
reliance*	6	C2	take place	8	B1			
renewable	5	C1	task* (n)	10	B2			

*These words are on the Academic Word List (AWL). The AWL is a list of the 570 most frequent word families in academic texts. It does not include the most frequent 2,000 words of English.

ACKNOWLEDGMENTS

The Authors and Publisher would like to acknowledge the teachers around the world who participated in the development of the second edition of *Pathways*.

A special thanks to our Advisory Board for their valuable input during the development of this series.

ADVISORY BOARD

Mahmoud Al Hosni, Modern College of Business and Science, Oman; **Safaa Al-Salim**, Kuwait University; **Laila Al-Qadhi**, Kuwait University; **Julie Bird**, RMIT University Vietnam; **Elizabeth Bowles**, Virginia Tech Language and Culture Institute, Blacksburg, VA; **Rachel Bricker**, Arizona State University, Tempe, AZ; **James Broadbridge**, J.F. Oberlin University, Tokyo; **Marina Broeder**, Mission College, Santa Clara, CA; **Shawn Campbell**, Hangzhou High School; **Trevor Carty**, James Cook University, Singapore; **Jindarat De Vleeschauwer**, Chiang Mai University; **Wai-Si El Hassan**, Prince Mohammad Bin Fahd University, Saudi Arabia; **Jennifer Farnell**, University of Bridgeport, Bridgeport, CT; **Rasha Gazzaz**, King Abdulaziz University, Saudi Arabia; **Keith Graziadei**, Santa Monica College, Santa Monica, CA; **Janet Harclerode**, Santa Monica Community College, Santa Monica, CA; **Anna Hasper**, TeacherTrain, UAE; **Phoebe Kamel Yacob Hindi**, Abu Dhabi Vocational Education and Training Institute, UAE; **Kuei-ping Hsu**, National Tsing Hua University; **Greg Jewell**, Drexel University, Philadelphia, PA; **Adisra Katib**, Chulalongkorn University Language Institute, Bangkok; **Wayne Kennedy**, LaGuardia Community College, Long Island City, NY; **Beth Koo**, Central Piedmont Community College, Charlotte, NC; **Denise Kray**, Bridge School, Denver, CO; **Chantal Kruger**, ILA Vietnam; **William P. Kyzner**, Fuyang AP Center; **Becky Lawrence**, Massachusetts International Academy, Marlborough, MA; **Deborah McGraw**, Syracuse University, NY; **Mary Moore**, University of Puerto Rico; **Raymond Purdy**, ELS Language Centers, Princeton, NJ; **Anouchka Rachelson**, Miami Dade College, Miami, FL; **Fathimah Razman**, Universiti Utara Malaysia; **Phil Rice**, University of Delaware ELI, Newark, DE; **Scott Rousseau**, American University of Sharjah, UAE; **Verna Santos-Nafrada**, King Saud University, Saudi Arabia; **Eugene Sidwell**, American Intercon Institute, Phnom Penh; **Gemma Thorp**, Monash University English Language Centre, Australia; **Matt Thurston**, University of Central Lancashire, UK; **Christine Tierney**, Houston Community College, Houston, TX; **Jet Robredillo Tonogbanua**, FPT University, Hanoi.

GLOBAL REVIEWERS

ASIA

Antonia Cavcic, Asia University, Tokyo; **Soyhan Egitim**, Tokyo University of Science; **Caroline Handley**, Asia University, Tokyo; **Patrizia Hayashi**, Meikai University, Urayasu; **Greg Holloway**, University of Kitakyushu; **Anne C. Ihata**, Musashino University, Tokyo; **Kathryn Mabe**, Asia University, Tokyo; **Frederick Navarro Bacala**, Yokohama City University; **Tyson Rode**, Meikai University, Urayasu; **Scott Shelton-Strong**, Asia University, Tokyo; **Brooks Slaybaugh**, Yokohama City University; **Susanto Sugiharto**, Sutomo Senior High School, Medan; **Andrew Zitzmann**, University of Kitakyushu.

LATIN AMERICA AND THE CARIBBEAN

Raul Bilini, ProLingua, Dominican Republic; **Alejandro Garcia**, Colegio Marcelina, Mexico; **Humberto Guevara**, Tec de Monterrey, Campus Monterrey, Mexico; **Romina Olga Planas**, Centro Cultural Paraguayo Americano, Paraguay; **Carlos Rico-Troncoso**, Pontificia Universidad Javeriana, Colombia; **Ialê Schetty**, Enjoy English, Brazil; **Aline Simoes**, Way To Go Private English, Brazil; **Paulo Cezar Lira Torres**, APenglish, Brazil; **Rosa Enilda Vasquez**, Swisher Dominicana, Dominican Republic; **Terry Whitty**, LDN Language School, Brazil.

MIDDLE EAST AND NORTH AFRICA

Susan Daniels, Kuwait University, Kuwait; **Mahmoud Mohammadi Khomeini**, Sokhane Ashna Language School, Iran; **Müge Lenbet**, Koç University, Turkey; **Robert Anthony Lowman**, Prince Mohammad bin Fahd University, Saudi Arabia; **Simon Mackay**, Prince Mohammad bin Fahd University, Saudi Arabia.

USA AND CANADA

Frank Abbot, Houston Community College, Houston, TX; **Hossein Aksari**, Bilingual Education Institute and Houston Community College, Houston, TX; **Sudie Allen-Henn**, North Seattle College, Seattle, WA; **Sharon Allie**, Santa Monica Community College, Santa Monica, CA; **Jerry Archer**, Oregon State University, Corvallis, OR; **Nicole Ashton**, Central Piedmont Community College, Charlotte, NC; **Barbara Barrett**, University of Miami, Coral Gables, FL; **Maria Bazan-Myrick**, Houston Community College, Houston, TX; **Rebecca Beal**, Colleges of Marin, Kentfield, CA; **Marlene Beck**, Eastern Michigan University, Ypsilanti, MI; **Michelle Bell**, University of Southern California, Los Angeles, CA; **Linda Bolet**, Houston Community College, Houston, TX; **Jenna Bollinger**, Eastern Michigan University, Ypsilanti, MI; **Monica Boney**, Houston Community College, Houston, TX; **Nanette Bouvier**, Rutgers University – Newark, Newark, NJ; **Nancy Boyer**, Golden West College, Huntington Beach, CA; **Lia Brenneman**, University of Florida English Language Institute, Gainesville, FL; **Colleen Brice**, Grand Valley State University, Allendale, MI; **Kristen Brown**, Massachusetts International Academy, Marlborough, MA; **Philip Brown**, Houston Community College, Houston, TX; **Dongmei Cao**, San Jose City College, San Jose, CA; **Molly Cheney**, University of Washington, Seattle, WA; **Emily Clark**, The University of Kansas, Lawrence, KS; **Luke Coffelt**, International English Center, Boulder, CO; **William C. Cole-French**, MCPHS University,

Boston, MA; **Charles Colson**, English Language Institute at Sam Houston State University, Huntsville, TX; **Lucy Condon**, Bilingual Education Institute, Houston, TX; **Janice Crouch**, Internexus Indiana, Indianapolis, IN; **Charlene Dandrow**, Virginia Tech Language and Culture Institute, Blacksburg, VA; **Loretta Davis**, Coastline Community College, Westminster, CA; **Marta Dmytrenko-Ahrabian**, Wayne State University, Detroit, MI; **Bonnie Duhart**, Houston Community College, Houston, TX; **Karen Eichhorn**, International English Center, Boulder, CO; **Tracey Ellis**, Santa Monica Community College, Santa Monica, CA; **Jennifer Evans**, University of Washington, Seattle, WA; **Marla Ewart**, Bilingual Education Institute, Houston, TX; **Rhoda Fagerland**, St. Cloud State University, St. Cloud, MN; **Kelly Montijo Fink**, Kirkwood Community College, Cedar Rapids, IA; **Celeste Flowers**, University of Central Arkansas, Conway, AR; **Kurtis Foster**, Missouri State University, Springfield, MO; **Rachel Garcia**, Bilingual Education Institute, Houston, TX; **Thomas Germain**, University of Colorado Boulder, Boulder, CO; **Claire Gimble**, Virginia International University, Fairfax, VA; **Marilyn Glazer-Weisner**, Middlesex Community College, Lowell, MA; **Amber Goodall**, South Piedmont Community College, Charlotte, NC; **Katya Goussakova**, Seminole State College of Florida, Sanford, FL; **Jane Granado**, Texas State University, San Marcos, TX; **Therea Hampton**, Mercer County Community College, West Windsor Township, NJ; **Jane Hanson**, University of Nebraska – Lincoln, Lincoln, NE; **Lauren Heather**, University of Texas at San Antonio, San Antonio, TX; **Jannette Hermina**, Saginaw Valley State University, Saginaw, MI; **Gail Hernandez**, College of Staten Island, Staten Island, NY; **Beverly Hobbs**, Clark University, Worcester, MA; **Kristin Homuth**, Language Center International, Southfield, MI; **Tim Hooker**, Campbellsville University, Campbellsville, KY; **Raylene Houck**, Idaho State University, Pocatello, ID; **Karen L. Howling**, University of Bridgeport, Bridgeport, CT; **Sharon Jaffe**, Santa Monica Community College, Santa Monica, CA; **Andrea Kahn**, Santa Monica Community College, Santa Monica, CA; **Eden Bradshaw Kaiser**, Massachusetts International Academy, Marlborough, MA; **Mandy Kama**, Georgetown University, Washington, D.C.; **Andrea Kaminski**, University of Michigan – Dearborn, Dearborn, MI; **Eileen Kramer**, Boston University CELOP, Brookline, MA; **Rachel Lachance**, University of New Hampshire, Durham, NH; **Janet Langon**, Glendale Community College, Glendale, CA; **Frances Le Grand**, University of Houston, Houston, TX; **Esther Lee**, California State University, Fullerton, CA; **Helen S. Mays Lefal**, American Learning Institute, Dallas, TX; **Oranit Limmaneeprasert**, American River College, Sacramento, CA; **Dhammika Liyanage**, Bilingual Education Institute, Houston, TX; **Emily Lodmer**, Santa Monica Community College, Santa Monica, CA; **Ari Lopez**, American Learning Institute, Dallas, TX; **Nichole Lukas**, University of Dayton, Dayton, OH; **Undarmaa Maamuujav**, California State University, Los Angeles, CA; **Diane Mahin**, University of Miami, Coral Gables, FL; **Melanie Majeski**, Naugatuck Valley Community College, Waterbury, CT; **Judy Marasco**, Santa Monica Community College, Santa Monica, CA; **Murray McMahan**, University of Alberta, Edmonton, AB, Canada; **Deirdre McMurtry**, University of Nebraska Omaha, Omaha, NE; **Suzanne Meyer**, University of Pittsburgh, Pittsburgh, PA; **Cynthia Miller**, Richland College, Dallas, TX; **Sara Miller**, Houston Community College, Houston, TX; **Gwendolyn Miraglia**, Houston Community College, Houston, TX; **Katie Mitchell**, International English Center, Boulder, CO; **Ruth Williams Moore**, University of Colorado Boulder, Boulder, CO; **Kathy Najafi**, Houston Community College, Houston, TX; **Sandra Navarro**, Glendale Community College, Glendale, CA; **Stephanie Ngom**, Boston University, Boston, MA; **Barbara Niemczyk**, University of Bridgeport, Bridgeport, CT; **Melody Nightingale**, Santa Monica Community College, Santa Monica, CA; **Alissa Olgun**, California Language Academy, Los Angeles, CA; **Kimberly Oliver**, Austin Community College, Austin, TX; **Steven Olson**, International English Center, Boulder, CO; **Fernanda Ortiz**, University of Arizona, Tucson, AZ; **Joel Ozretich**, University of Washington, Seattle, WA; **Erin Pak**, Schoolcraft College, Livonia, MI; **Geri Pappas**, University of Michigan – Dearborn, Dearborn, MI; **Eleanor Paterson**, Erie Community College, Buffalo, NY; **Sumeeta Patnaik**, Marshall University, Huntington, WV; **Mary Peacock**, Richland College, Dallas, TX; **Kathryn Porter**, University of Houston, Houston, TX; **Eileen Prince**, Prince Language Associates, Newton Highlands, MA; **Marina Ramirez**, Houston Community College, Houston, TX; **Laura Ramm**, Michigan State University, East Lansing, MI; **Chi Rehg**, University of South Florida, Tampa, FL; **Cyndy Reimer**, Douglas College, New Westminster, BC, Canada; **Sydney Rice**, Imperial Valley College, Imperial, CA; **Lynnette Robson**, Mercer University, Macon, GA; **Helen E. Roland**, Miami Dade College, Miami, FL; **Maria Paula Carreira Rolim**, Southeast Missouri State University, Cape Girardeau, MO; **Jill Rolston-Yates**, Texas State University, San Marcos, TX; **David Ross**, Houston Community College, Houston, TX; **Rachel Scheiner**, Seattle Central College, Seattle, WA; **John Schmidt**, Texas Intensive English Program, Austin, TX; **Mariah Schueman**, University of Miami, Coral Gables, FL; **Erika Shadburne**, Austin Community College, Austin, TX; **Mahdi Shamsi**, Houston Community College, Houston, TX; **Osha Sky**, Highline College, Des Moines, WA; **William Slade**, University of Texas, Austin, TX; **Takako Smith**, University of Nebraska – Lincoln, Lincoln, NE; **Barbara Smith-Palinkas**, Hillsborough Community College, Tampa, FL; **Paula Snyder**, University of Missouri, Columbia, MO; **Mary Evelyn Sorrell**, Bilingual Education Institute, Houston, TX; **Kristen Stauffer**, International English Center, Boulder, CO; **Christina Stefanik**, The Language Company, Toledo, OH; **Cory Stewart**, University of Houston, Houston, TX; **Laurie Stusser-McNeill**, Highline College, Des Moines, WA; **Tom Sugawara**, University of Washington, Seattle, WA; **Sara Sulko**, University of Missouri, Columbia, MO; **Mark Sullivan**, University of Colorado Boulder, Boulder, CO; **Olivia Szabo**, Boston University, Boston, MA; **Amber Tallent**, University of Nebraska Omaha, Omaha, NE; **Amy Tate**, Rice University, Houston, TX; **Aya C. Tiacoh**, Bilingual Education Institute, Houston, TX; **Troy Tucker**, Florida SouthWestern State College, Fort Myers, FL; **Anne Tyoan**, Savannah College of Art and Design, Savannah, GA; **Michael Vallee**, International English Center, Boulder, CO; **Andrea Vasquez**, University of Southern Maine, Portland, ME; **Jose Vasquez**, University of Texas Rio Grande Valley, Edinburgh, TX; **Maureen Vendeville**, Savannah Technical College, Savannah, GA; **Melissa Vervinck**, Oakland University, Rochester, MI; **Adriana Villarreal**, Universidad Nacional Autonoma de Mexico, San Antonio, TX; **Summer Webb**, International English Center, Boulder, CO; **Mercedes Wilson-Everett**, Houston Community College, Houston, TX; **Lora Yasen**, Tokyo International University of America, Salem, OR; **Dennis Yommer**, Youngstown State University, Youngstown, OH; **Melojeane (Jolene) Zawilinski**, University of Michigan – Flint, Flint, MI.

CREDITS

Photos

Cover, iii KiskaMedia/iStock/Getty Images, **iv** (from top to bottom) Thomas Mangelsen/Minden Pictures, Kenneth Garrett/National Geographic Creative, Ricardo Ribas/Alamy Stock Photo, Anadolu Agency/Getty Images, Sergio Pitamitz/National Geographic Creative, **1** Thomas Mangelsen/Minden Pictures, **2** Thomas Marent/Minden Pictures, **5** Michael Nichols/National Geographic Creative, **6** Pressmaster/Shutterstock, **7** hypergurl/Getty Images, **11** Visions of America/Getty Images, **14–15** (t) Michael Fay/National Geographic Creative, **15** (br) Michael Nichols/National Geographic Creative, **16** Michael Poliza/National Geographic Creative, **21** Joel Sartore/National Geographic Creative, **25** Kenneth Garrett/National Geographic Creative, **26** (l) Razvan Ionut Dragomirescu/Shutterstock, **27** (l, tr, c, br) Jason Treat/National Geographic Creative, **29** Kenneth Garrett/National Geographic Creative, **30** Dan Suzio/Getty Images, **31** Kazuhiko Sano/National Geographic Creative, **35** imageBROKER/Alamy Stock Photo, **38–39** Kenneth Garrett/National Geographic Creative, **40** Kenneth Garrett/National Geographic Creative, **49** Ricardo Ribas/Alamy Stock Photo, **50–51** Mike Theiss/National Geographic Creative, **53** Robert Harding/Alamy Stock Photo, **54** Neilson Barnard/Getty Images, **55** John Tomanio/National Geographic, **57** Wangwukong/Getty Images, **58** Cengage Learning, **59** Graeme Robertson/Eyevine/Redux, **62** Michael Loccisano/Getty Images, **63** Rolf Hicker Photography/Alamy Stock Photo, **73** Anadolu Agency/Getty Images, **77** Tom Lynn/Getty Images, **78** © TEAM Network, **79** Glenn Bartley/BIA/Minden Pictures/Getty Images, **81** Joel Sartore/National Geographic Photo Ark/National Geographic Creative, **83** Zachary West/Army National Guard/Getty Images, **86** Rich Reid/National Geographic Creative, **87** Hernan Canellas/National Geographic Image Collection, **88–89** Hernan Canellas/National Geographic Creative, **90** Alejandro Tumas/National Geographic Creative, **92** Hernan Canellas/National Geographic Creative, **99** Sergio Pitamitz/National Geographic Creative, **100–101** Sean Pavone/Alamy Stock Photo, **103** Andrew Bain/Getty Images, **104** (tl) Mark Thiessen/National Geographic Creative, **104–105** Thomas Trutschel/Getty Images, **107** Norman Wharton/Alamy Stock Photo, **109** Jeff Greenberg/Getty Images, **112** Robert Harding Picture Library/National Geographic Creative, **113** © 3 Sisters Adventure, **114** Richard Nowitz/National Geographic Creative, **115** Jason Edwards/National Geographic Creative, **248** Mike Theiss/National Geographic Creative

Texts/Sources

5–7 Adapted from "Office Jungle Mirrors Primate Behavior" by Brian Handwerk: http://news.nationalgeographic.com/news/2005/09/0923_050923_ape_office.html; **14–16** Adapted from "Kings of the Hill?" by Virginia Morrell: NGM November 2002, and "Chimp "Girls" Play With "Dolls" Too—First Wild Evidence" by Brain Handwerk: http://news.nationalgeographic.com/news/2010/09/101220-chimpanzees-play-nature-nurture-science-animals-evolution/; **29–31** Based on information from "Crime-Fighting Leech Fingers Perp": http://news.nationalgeographic.com/news/2009/10/091020-leech-robber-dna-video-ap.html, "Animal DNA Becoming Crucial CSI Clue": http://news.nationalgeographic.com/news/2006/12/061212-animals-CSI_2.html, and "Iceman Autopsy" by Stephen S. Hall: NGM November 2011; **38–40** Adapted from "King Tut's Family Secrets" by Zahi Hawass: NGM September 2010; **53–55** Adapted from "City Solutions" by Robert Kunzig: NGM December 2011, **62–64** Adapted from "Urban Visionary: One on One" by Keith Bellows: https://www.nationalgeographic.com/travel/traveler-magazine/one-on-one/urban-visionary/; **77–79** Adapted from "Scientists Seek Foolproof Signal to Predict Earthquakes" by Richard A. Lovett: https://news.nationalgeographic.com/news/2013/01/04-earthquakees-defy-prediction-efforts/, and "Birds May Have Sensed Severe Storms Days in Advance" by Carrie Arnold: https://news.nationalgeographic.com/news/2014/12/141218-birds-weather-tornadoes-science-animals-environment/, and additional information from "Wild Animals Can Help 'Predict' Earthquakes, Scientists Say": nbcnews.com, March 24, 2015; **86–90** Adapted from "When Yellowstone Explodes" by Joel Achenbach: NGM August 2009; **103–105** Adapted from "One on One: Jonathan Tourtellot" by Daniel R. Westergren: National Geographic Traveler November 2006; **112–114** Based on information from "3 Sisters Adventure Trekking": http://www.3sistersadventure.com/, and "Australia Through Aboriginal Eyes" by Francis Wilkins: http://news.nationalgeographic.com/news/2004/12/1210_041210_travel_australia.html

NGM = National Geographic Magazine

Maps and Infographics

26–27 Jason Treat/National Geographic Creative, **51** 5W Infographics, **64** 5W Infographics; source: Urban Observatory, **74–75** National Geographic Creative; source: Münchener Rückversicherungs-Gesellschaft, **100** (bl) 5W Infographics; source: Mastercard Global Destinations Cities Index 2016, **101** (br) 5W Infographics; source: Mastercard Global Destinations Cities Index 2016

INDEX OF EXAM SKILLS AND TASKS

The activities in *Pathways Reading, Writing, and Critical Thinking* develop **key reading skills** needed for success on standardized tests such as TOEFL® and IELTS. In addition, many of the activities provide useful exam practice because they are similar to **common question types** in these tests.

Key Reading Skills	IELTS	TOEFL®	Page(s)
Recognizing vocabulary from context	✓	✓	4, 9, 13, 18, 28, 42, 52, 66, 76, 81, 92, 116, 131, 140, 164, 188, 202, 227
Identifying main ideas	✓	✓	8, 10, 17, 32, 41, 57, 80, 106, 115, 132, 139, 154, 163, 178, 202, 211, 226, 235
Identifying supporting ideas	✓	✓	9, 10, 17, 18, 56, 57, 92, 107, 130, 139, 187, 202, 211, 235
Scanning for details	✓	✓	17, 32, 41, 42, 65, 80, 130, 139, 163, 164, 179, 202, 204, 211, 212, 228, 235
Making inferences	✓	✓	33, 42, 66, 81, 91, 155, 227
Recognizing pronoun references	✓	✓	82, 188
Understanding charts and infographics	✓		58, 66, 91, 130, 131, 155, 164, 202, 211

Common Question Types	IELTS	TOEFL®	Page(s)
Multiple choice	✓	✓	8, 65, 81, 91, 106, 154, 164, 187, 211, 226, 236
Completion (notes, diagram, chart)	✓		17, 18, 34, 41, 65, 80, 92, 107, 108, 116, 187, 212
Completion (summary)	✓		8, 80, 91, 163, 178, 187, 226
Short answer	✓		9, 33, 56, 66, 80, 91, 92, 107, 116, 131, 139, 140, 154, 163, 164, 179, 202, 203, 211, 235
Matching headings / information	✓		8, 32, 41, 56, 65, 115, 178, 235
Categorizing (Matching features)	✓	✓	8, 18, 32, 66, 106, 115, 139, 155
True / False / Not Given	✓		32, 41, 80, 154
Prose summary		✓	56, 130
Rhetorical purpose		✓	8, 178

Level 3 of *Pathways Reading, Writing, and Critical Thinking* also develops **key writing skills** needed for exam success.

Key Writing Skills	Unit(s)
Writing strong body paragraphs	1, 4, 7, 9, 10
Writing a strong introduction and conclusion	3, 10
Expressing and justifying opinions	6, 7
Giving reasons and examples	1, 5, 6, 7, 8, 9
Paraphrasing / Summarizing	2
Making comparisons	1
Describing problems and solutions	3
Explaining a process	4
Expressing agreement and disagreement	6, 9
Describing a graph or chart	6

Pathways	CEFR	IELTS Band	TOEFL® Score
Level 4	C1	6.5–7.0	81–100
Level 3	**B2**	**5.5–6.0**	**51–80**
Level 2	B1–B2	4.5–5.0	31–50
Level 1	A2–B1	0–4.0	0–30
Foundations	A1–A2		